GARDENING
VERTICALLY

For information about permission to reproduce
selections from this book, write to Permissions,
W. W. Norton & Company, Inc., 500 Fifth Avenue,
New York, NY 10110

For information about special discounts for bulk purchases, please contact
W. W. Norton
Special Sales at specialsales@wwnorton.com or 800-233-4830

Illustrations: Dominique Klecka
Book design: Iris Glon

Manufacturing by KHL Printing Co Pte Ltd
Electronic production: Joe Lops
Production manager: Leeann Graham

Library of Congress Cataloging-in-Publication Data

Vialard, Noémie.
    [Jardinons à la verticale! English]
    Gardening vertically : 24 ideas for creating your own green walls / Noémie
Vialard with Méline Vialard ; preface by Patrick Blanc ; illustrations by
Dominique Klecka ; translated by Bryan M. Woy.
        p. cm.
    Originally published in French as: Jardinons à la verticale!
    Includes bibliographical references and index.
    ISBN 978-0-393-73370-9 (pbk.)
    1. Vertical gardening. I. Vialard, Méline. II. Title. III. Title: 24 ideas for
creating your own green walls. IV. Title: Twenty-four ideas for creating
your own green walls.
    SB463.5.V5313 2012
    635'.048—dc23
                                            2011036453
    ISBN: 978-0-393-73370-9 (pbk.)

W. W. Norton & Company, Inc., 500 Fifth Avenue, New York, N.Y. 10110
                        www.wwnorton.com
W. W. Norton & Company Ltd., Castle House, 75/76 Wells Street, London
W1T 3QT

0 9 8 7 6 5 4 3 2 1

GARDENING VERTICALLY

24 Ideas for Creating Your Own Green Walls

Noémie Vialard

with **Méline Vialard**

Foreword by Patrick Blanc

Translated by Bryan M. Woy

Illustrations by Dominique Klecka

W. W. Norton & Company
New York • London

4

CONTENTS

A big thank you . . .

to Patrick Blanc
to Pascal Heni
to Jérôme Niort
to Thierry Chastagnier
to Jean Luc Le Gouallec
to Géraldine Bouclon

to Frédérique Chavance, my French publisher, patient and always cheerful, despite the delays . . .

and of course to Méline. If she had not written all the technical parts, I would have given up on this book . . .

FOREWORD Patrick Blanc

She's done it! She's written this book that invites us all to look upward and admire the plants that are above us, which sometimes dominate us and which will never be crushed under our feet: grown vertically, plants become free, free as we ourselves dream of once more becoming. If our friendship has gone on getting stronger, for almost thirty years now, it is because Noémie and I share this fascination, tinged with respect, for plants. Of course, Noémie, with her wild femininity, touches, smells, picks, and eats them, while for me they are objects of desire in which I immerse myself and which I try to understand and tame by attempting to recreate their native habitat.

In the 1960s, when I started tinkering around with growing media to maintain philodendrons over my aquarium, I did not, of course, imagine that this approach, designed to be ecological (purifying the water by absorbing nitrates from the metabolism of the fish), would result, thirty years later, in my collaborating with leading architects to cover urban facades. Most of my highest vertical gardens currently reach 98 to 131 feet (30–40 m), that is to say the height of the forest canopy, as we have observed it during missions of the *Radeau des Cimes* (Canopy Raft) project. This height therefore represents a reference point in our imaginations and is probably why passersby feel transported to a natural world when confronted with a vertical garden. What, then, will the reference points be for the vertical gardens that will cover skyscrapers?

But when vertical gardens are only a few meters tall, they tend to conjure up the atmosphere of small forest canyons, of caves, of the edges of waterfalls, or of the Mediterranean garrigue. It is on this scale that Noémie invites you to create vertical gardens—a return to when I was fifteen years old, but with all the fruits of experiments and tests done over many years. Noémie is familiar with all the steps involved, and for this reason is able to explain (with the help of her daughter Méline's very precise and light pen) how you can create, in a reliable and lasting way, your own wall. Of course, Noémie indulges her sensuality with her own choice of species, which goes well beyond those that grow naturally on vertical surfaces, but she knows them well, her beloved plants, and I am sure that by following her we will discover completely new aspects of the vertical garden. So put down your spades and rakes for a while, and get out your drills and staplers: they will plunge you into a whole new world!

PREFACE Noémie Vialard

Garlands, friezes, embroidery . . . climbing plants, those lovely acrobats, have always been with us: ivy running up the trunks of forest trees; bindweed irresistibly attracted by even the smallest plants; wild clematis adorning hedgerows with its creeping stems covered with feathery fruits . . . Since time immemorial, gardeners have been copying nature, installing vines and climbers to adorn a facade, to embellish an arbor, or to hide a wall, pole, or post.

Even when I was very young, I loved what has since become my passion and my profession: the countryside, and the wild and barely domesticated garden plants that grow in it. Wild-looking climbers fitted very well in this setting. I can still remember the glass awning over the front door of my grandparents' house, covered all over with delicious rumpled-looking roses, the gorgeous Virginia creeper that helpfully hid the neighbor's horrible cinderblock wall, and the fragrant cascades of honeysuckle that accompanied lunches under the gazebo. I can't have been more than eight years old. Then later I discovered plants that lived on almost nothing, growing in the interstices of old walls, forcing me to look up. I always enjoy these pretty things, apparently living on air, enlivening walls beside seaside lanes. I had, of course, found mosses and ferns inside the damp caves in the cliffs, taking advantage of the moisture to spread and multiply. I would nibble the rock samphire that clung to the rocks of the Brittany coast. By this time I had realized that plants could grow without being planted in the ground—basic reasoning, which many had already noticed well before I did. Nobody, however, had ever thought of deliberately cultivating plants in this way.

It was with observations just like these, particularly those made in tropical forests, that Patrick Blanc opened up a whole new way of thinking thirty years ago, by creating a concept in which plants grew on vertical surfaces. The first time I saw the wall he had created, over twenty years ago in the apartment he then occupied in the 13th arrondissement, I was totally amazed by the way the plants grew and by the resulting atmosphere.

A new step had been taken, and now we could all start creating our own vertical gardens—without, of course, forgetting all those beautiful and extravagant climbing plants.

When I chose the specific plants that are showcased in the examples in this book, I was thinking of different situations and contexts: modern terraces, old-fashioned gardens, balconies . . . It is up to you to copy or take inspiration from them.

INTRODUCTION

THE HISTORY OF VERTICAL GARDENING

Gardeners have known for a very long time that walls are not barriers, but allies that give them more space and extra surfaces for plants, whether they choose a natural look or give free play to their fantasy. Curtains of greenery, floral traceries, plant sculptures . . . you could create almost anything, simply by planting in the soil at the foot of the wall. But Patrick Blanc's Green Wall concept has dramatically changed the history of vertical gardening, and it paved the way for many new techniques, now that we can plant directly "on" the walls!

FROM CLASSICAL GARDENING
TO GREEN WALLS

Until thirty years ago, only vines and other climbers were available to us for vertical gardening. Then Patrick Blanc developed his wonderful invention: the Green Wall, or vertical garden. This concept is the result of a long series of tests and trials through which he gradually moved forward to his final design. Today we can admire these exciting creations all over the world.

CLIMBING PLANTS:
THE CLASSICS!

Climbing plants, whether they are shrubs with twining branches or annual herbaceous climbers, grow in a number of different ways. If these plants do not find an artificial or natural support, they creep along the ground. In order to grow vertically, they must be able to lean, climb, cling, and twine.

Certain plants lend themselves well to trellising; sometimes this is easy, but sometimes we need to employ special growing techniques.

Gardeners have been taking advantage of these observations for thousands of years, using the characteristics of these plants to decorate, trim, or conceal natural or artificial supports. The trellised pergola was invented four thousand years ago, as a support for grape vines. Although the word "trellis," meaning "lattice used to support vines," did not appear until the sixteenth century, the art of the trellis, and therefore of vertical planting, emerged as an architectural element around 2000 BC.

The style of gardens changed over the centuries, and various structures were devised, with specific meanings: if pergolas encourage the idea of going for a walk, arbors, gazebos, and arches or cradles of greenery suggest that we are being invited to contemplate and to rest. Obelisks, tripods, teepees, pillars, and columns rise up from a landscape, or even from a flowerbed or shrubbery, to give the scene a vertical surge, a

striking visual effect, an obvious strength. Climbing plants love to grow on supports like these.

We espalier fruit trees to increase their production and for the beauty of their sculpted branches, which enliven the blind walls they grow against.

The twentieth century saw a fashion for growing climbing plants through trees: roses, wisteria, clematis, etc. But the largest plants cannot exceed 50 feet (15 m) in height, so using them to mask or adorn the walls of skyscrapers is impossible.

The twenty-first century will go down in history as the time when Patrick Blanc's Green Walls arrived . . .

Opposite: The rose 'Paul Transom' can grow 15 feet (4.5 m) high.

Above: A wisteria is capable of covering a large area.

THE BIRTH OF THE GREEN WALL

Plant lovers, particularly in France, are all familiar with Patrick Blanc's green lock of hair, glimpsed at a plant festival, seen at a conference or in a television program filmed at the other end of the world. Patrick, a botanist and researcher at the CNRS, the French national research institute, is above all a practical man. For over thirty-five years, he has explored the rainforest to study the plant life that grows underneath the forest canopy. He is one of those scholars who travel all over the world, curious about everything, and whose writings and work flow directly from their research into Nature.

The Quai Branly Museum (Paris, 15th arrondissement), designed in collaboration with the architect Jean Nouvel in 2004. Nearly 900 square yards of vertical greenery.

His enthusiasm, his ability to tell people about botany and make it understandable to everyone and the Green Walls he installs on every continent have made him famous. But how did this concept come about? Let's go back in time . . .

A youthful passion

As a child, Patrick's point of reference was not the garden but the aquarium. Thus it was in water that he first started assembling and arranging plants, and he has retained a taste for aquatic plants ever since. At the age of five, he stood in awe in front of the large tropical aquarium in the family doctor's waiting room. Living in the city, with no concept of the country-side, he was fascinated by this living world, with fish and plants mingled together. Soon, his parents gave him his own aquarium. He observed and learned, becoming familiar early on with the concept of ecosystems.

His first steps toward the Green Wall were taken near the waterfalls in the Bois de Boulogne, where he could see mosses.

Searching for the ideal growing medium

Naturally, he turned to scientific studies. While studying for an undergraduate degree in Natural Science, he went with a friend to Thailand and Malaysia. There, seeing the plants cov-ering the rocks, surviving on just the water droplets splash-ing off waterfalls, he understood that plants are able to grow at any height off the ground. Patrick dreamed of reproducing what he had seen in the tropical forests: plants that grow on vertical surfaces, clinging to rock walls or tree trunks. Each time he came back to his small apartment in Suresnes, he experimented with different types of materials to copy nature and set up vertical supports for plants he had observed on his expeditions. Thus he transformed a small waterfall that he had earlier cobbled together over his aquarium, extending it right up to the ceiling by adding a wooden plank covered with a sealant. Some rather perfunctory irrigation was installed, employing wire mesh and sphagnum moss. He went on trying to get as close as possible to what he had observed in nature, because over the years he had been traveling and studying more and more.

He very quickly understood that the key was to develop the ideal growing medium: thin, lightweight, and rot-resistant. Once this had been done, he just needed to install a very simple irrigation system to provide water and nutrients. His first test consisted of a wall of sphagnum moss trapped between the wire mesh and the wooden board. But the sphagnum moss did not grow well in the hard water of Paris, and the whole arrangement was unsatisfactory, as the moss tended to clump together into a solid mass. When Patrick replaced it with blocks of compacted peat, he again came up against problems of the material massing together. Coconut fiber and rock wool seemed more appropriate, but sustainability was a problem, as both materials deteriorate over time. He concluded that he should try to imitate nature by devising a layer that would be only a few millimeters thick, nonbiodegradable, and light enough not to clump together, in which mosses and microorganisms could develop spontaneously.

The turning point of this research came with an unexpected discovery: in a vacant lot, he observed an old floor cloth covered with moss, algae, and small plants. He hurried home and stapled a floor cloth onto his wooden plank, and observed what happened. It turned out to be a perfect living medium, encouraging root development and quickly becoming covered with moss and algae. But the cotton cloth itself decomposed too quickly. However, in 1977 he discovered the irrigation matting used in greenhouses. This matting has the same qualities as cotton cloth, but with a big plus: it does not rot, as it is made up of fragments of recycled synthetic fabrics, and thus the sustainability of the installation is ensured.

Irrigation matting

Also called, among other things, horticultural felt, irrigation lining, and mat medium, irrigation matting has long been used in horticulture to maintain humidity between pots in greenhouses. It has outstanding qualities that make it the material of choice for Patrick Blanc's Green Walls. It is a nonwoven synthetic, making it lightweight and rotproof; it can adapt to changes in the climate and it has a strong capillary power that ensures the even distribution of water and minerals.

Looking for the right support for the felt

Patrick conducted many trials and experiments before discovering the perfect material on which to fix the irrigation matting (felt). At first he tried to imitate the trunks of the trees on which epiphytes grow, fixing the felt onto marine-quality

fiberboard. But these fiberboard panels turned out to last for only a few years. He continued searching, and finally came across expanded PVC foam. This foamed plastic material has three major advantages: it is waterproof, it is light, and it does not crack when you drill holes in it for the screws, nails, and staples that hold the different elements and plants in place.

Now, after thirty years, his basic concept has been fully developed, and with his enormous knowledge of botany he can devote plenty of time to being creative and to trying to reproduce in an urban setting what he has observed in the natural environment.

Living in the natural world

Patrick Blanc's oldest Green Wall is still alive and doing well: set up indoors almost thirty years ago in his apartment in the 13th arrondissement of Paris, it was transported by moving van to the house in Créteil where Patrick lived for many years. His sister, who took over the lease of the house, has inherited it.

More recently Patrick has been living in a house in the Paris suburbs, on the far side of the ring road. From the outside it looks just like thousands of other houses. Once we go through the porch, however, we find ourselves in a universe filled with plants and music.

The house is surrounded by corridors on two levels, and there are steps here and there leading us to other levels in between. In the middle is a courtyard surrounded by massive walls of plants; then, opening onto the large living room, Patrick's office, called the "Christarium" because you walk on water: the floor is a huge aquarium, in which you can glimpse fish and aquatic plants. A skylight lights up the two gigantic walls, which are lined with mosses, ferns, and extravagant lianas. Lizards and birds live freely in this magical world. Nearby, Pascal, at the piano, interprets a text by Dante that he has set to music. He is trying it out; possibly for his new album. Singing is the botanist's other great passion. Just as well: his companion, Pascal Heni ("Pascal of Bollywood"), is a singer. Patrick also likes singing songs himself. Just like that, without warning, anywhere, whenever he feels like it, he sings one of the songs associated with his favorite star, Zarah Leander.

It is impossible to leave without visiting the "lab," a room lit by spotlights and walls of glass that multiply the light. Here Patrick pampers the seedlings and cuttings brought back from his explorations. Because even though he is invited all over the world to explain the art of vertical gardening, even though he regularly intervenes as "inventor" in projects for new Green Walls, Patrick still continues to explore rainforests, never tiring of observing how a root grows over a trunk, or what method a plant uses to attach itself, to feed, and to live with, and sometimes even imitate, its neighbors.

Now that the basic concept has been perfected, the development of Patrick's work on Green Walls has been toward trying to recreate, through his observations and his imagination, his endless forays into natural environments around the world.

The plantings on the walls
surrounding the patio of
Patrick's house are only
a few months old. What
exuberance there is
already!

GREEN WALLS BY PATRICK BLANC
... AND HIS FOLLOWERS

When Patrick Blanc began to adorn the walls of his apartment, and then the garden of the house in Créteil, the concept was known only to his friends. It was the world of contemporary art, rather than the world of gardens, that first became interested in his work, through two exhibitions: *In visu, in situ*, in Albi, and *Être Nature* at the Cartier Foundation in Paris.

WALLS ALL OVER THE WORLD

Three milestones paved the way for Patrick's walls to flourish all over the world:

1994 • Jean-Paul Pigeat, the creator of the Chaumont-sur-Loire Garden Festival (who has now unfortunately passed away), after seeing some of Patrick's achievements, offered to present one of his Walls at the Festival, and France discovered them for the first time.

2001 • Andrée Putman, the famous interior designer, believed that these creations would be compatible with large surfaces. Why not create a wall 100 feet (30 m) high, in the courtyard of the Pershing Hall hotel in Paris? Thus this incredible (and so simple) concept was brought to the attention of the whole world.

2004 • Patrick worked with the architect Jean Nouvel to create the Green Walls of the Quai Branly Museum in Paris: an enormous green wall of 900 square yards. Acceptance is complete!

Many architects have since called upon his

Max Juvénal Bridge,
Aix-en-Provence (2008)

skills, among them Jean Nouvel, Kazuyo Sejima, Jacques Herzog, and Pierre de Meuron.

Indoors or outdoors, Patrick's creations multiply over countries and continents, always different depending on each region's vegetation and climate. From the Museum of Contemporary Art in Kanazawa (Japan), through arches and bridges, to car parks, towers, huge shopping malls, and train stations . . . in New York, Osaka, Sydney, Taipei, Tokyo, Bangkok, Delhi . . .

DESIGN THAT IS BOTH BOTANICAL AND ARTISTIC

Patrick uses many different species (up to four hundred for the Caixa Forum in Madrid), but only those that grow wild on slopes, cliffs, trunks, or branches. Priority is given to arranging them in an ecological sequence: the top of a wall is more exposed to sunlight, wind, and temperature fluctuations than the lower parts, so for the upper part he tends to favor species that grow at the tops of cliffs, with woodland species planted below. He also takes account of the adult development of each species, as a vertical garden must be beautiful when it is created, of course, along sloping

The Green Wall inspires other artists

Designer? Landscape architect? Gardener? Craftsman? Artist? Richard Dhennin is all of these things at once.

If he has drawn inspiration from Patrick Blanc's walls, he does not copy them. He designs, builds, and maintains installations for green spaces, terrace, and balconies, which may be for individuals, landscape designers, or local authorities. He combines the art of topiary with that of vertical gardening: an entirely new and different way of presenting plants. He is both a creative artist and a technician, with his own personal approach to the world of gardens. In 2009, in front of the Hotel de Ville in Paris, passersby were able to discover "compost columns" dedicated to insects, consisting of columns filled with green waste, mulch, and shredded tree prunings. These columns, with plants growing from them, allowed insects to nest in peace right in the heart of the city.

Végéforme website:
http://vegeforme.blogspot.com.

Opposite: 'Green Symphony' at the Concert Hall in Taipei, Taiwan, 2007.

My own favorites . . .

I have a penchant for the Wall at the Caixa Forum Museum (above) in Madrid. This gigantic work really brought home to me the fact that Patrick, in addition to being an outstanding botanist, was also an artist. The wall is a living painting, constantly evolving with exuberance and grace, according to the seasons, changing its appearance as different plants come into flower. It is a work of art in itself!

I find the Wall in the Rue d'Alsace (left), in Paris, tremendously impressive. It brings a dreary neighborhood, located between the Gare de l'Est and the Gare du Nord, out of its isolation. The planted surface of about 16,000 square feet (1,500 m²) is twice that of the Quai Branly, and it is located opposite rehabilitated buildings formerly belonging to SNCF, the French national railway company. As the street is very narrow, there is a stunning "canyon" effect.

To discover all these walls, visit the website: www.murvegetalpatrickblanc.com.

fault lines. He plays around with shades and contrasts, concentrating on the texture, sheen, and color of the foliage, taking into consideration, of course, the structure and habit of each plant.

FOLLOWERS OF GREEN WALLS

Like all great creators, Patrick has shown others the way; gardeners, landscape architects, artists, craftsmen, and artisans have all been inspired by his plant walls . . . and so much the better!

Until recently nobody had ever thought of gardening vertically in quite that way, but for the past five years the success of Green Walls has given plenty of ideas to a large number of "followers."

Unfortunately most of their techniques are unreliable and tend more toward the gadget. The size, weight, and strength of the structure, the properties of the substrate, the selection of plants, the systems for providing water and nutrients, the exposure, the upkeep . . . all have to be taken into account in order to make these vertical adventures permanent and to avoid their ending in failure.

The purchase of a "ready-made" green wall carries no guarantee of durability when you install it where you live. Before you fall for one of these modular elements, you need to have a good idea of where you want to go; and if you want to decorate a large area, you should ask to see one already in place in someone else's home.

There are smaller, less ambitious kits available on the market, which allow you to grow plants vertically and offer opportunities to present and cultivate them in many different ways; these open up many new green decorative possibilities.

Opposite:
Upper photo: Caixa Forum Museum, Madrid, Spain (2007).

Lower photo: Rue d'Alsace, Paris, 10th arrondissement (2008).

Below: Siam Paragon Shopping Center, Bangkok, Thailand (2005).

PATRICK BLANC'S VERTICAL GARDEN

There is no improvisation involved nowadays when the botanist Patrick Blanc creates his vertical gardens. Choosing and arranging the different species, holding the fine substrate in a vertical position, fixing and growing the plants, reducing weight to a minimum, and sealing the wall for maximum durability—all are the result of many years of experimentation to find the right materials.

BUILD YOUR OWN LITTLE WALL

Do you have the urge to create a small green wall of your own? It's easier than you might think if you are fairly good with your hands. If you have a little common sense and patience, and you are reasonably handy, then why not have a go? You may even feel tempted to let your imagination run wild; why not add a frame or some pretty gutters to your wall?

THE STORY OF MY LITTLE WALL OF AROMATIC PLANTS

First of all, I will tell you how my little wall of aromatic plants came about. I had dreamed about it for years . . . and when, four years ago, I moved to Brittany, Patrick Blanc immediately said to me, while we were walking around the garden: "What you need is a Green Wall—containing just aromatic plants, because your love of plants comes mainly through sensual pleasure. You look at them, you touch them, you smell them, and you eat them! And what's more, a wall made of

this kind of plant has never existed before: it will be the first." Of course, I was transported by this idea . . . but stayed discreet about it for the time being.

Over the months I worked on my new garden, the way I like to do it, that is to say in a very "country" way, mixing cultivated plants with wild plants from the local area. Climbing plants had taken over the trees, walls, and fences, forming a cocoon—"my" cocoon! But in the middle of this world of mine that was taking shape, there was an eyesore: the cinderblock wall of a small outbuilding, just too ugly for words! This eyesore would quickly be hidden, that very same year, by the creation of a Green Wall.

Composing "mini" green walls is an exercise in style, which should reflect both the gardener's personality and the environment. This is how it is with mine: it melts into my garden and also helps me to satisfy my appetite! Patrick chose the plants and drew up the plan to suit my tastes and my own way of understanding and loving nature.

He explained to one of my close friends and neighbors, Jérôme, how to put the structure in place and install the pump. Jérôme, who is both efficient and energetic, put everything together in no time at all.

Patrick drew up the plan for the green wall, selecting plants from the catalog of the Arom'antique nursery—and I myself added two or three fine and beautiful plants that I particularly wanted to the list and had them all delivered to my house. This wall of 190 square feet (18 m²) is composed of 350 plants of 80 different species and varieties: mints, *Agastache*, sages, thymes, wormwoods, tansies, lavenders, germanders, hyssops, *Santolina*, micromerias, bee balms, savories, catnips, barberries, oreganos, woodruffs, *Acinos*, deadnettles, *Cedronella*, curry plant (*Helichrysum italicum*), and more. There are over fifteen varieties of thyme, for example, planted in groups of five.

Thierry, a very old friend who looks after the maintenance of some of Patrick's Green Walls, came to do the "stapling." Jérôme and I spent a memorable sunny day in late June with him. Within hours, the wall had been totally transformed.

Aromatic plants close at hand, for flavoring dishes, making all kinds of herb teas, concocting herb salads, perfuming the house . . . *Santolina*, sage, *Agastache*, thyme, rosemary, wormwood, savory . . . 350 plants of 80 species and varieties in less than 200 square feet!

What a dope!

Stupidly, I did not take enough care when I bought the programmer: it could not be triggered more than three times a day. So I was forced to buy another one, which can be programmed to go off for three minutes up to six times a day in summer.

In November, I do not water more than three times a day, and in winter, just twice. And I cut off the water altogether when it freezes. These cycles will be different from region to region, and depending on the location of the wall. I had to fumble around a bit at the beginning before I found the right rhythm. Next year, the plants will be well established, and perhaps I will only need to water them four or five times a day. Wait and see . . .

Three months later, when Patrick came back, the wall was completely covered and in full bloom, producing a riot of herbal teas, fragrances, and different flavors to add to dishes. Since then, I have been concocting any number of herb salads, without having to bend down to pick them! I have everything at my fingertips. Passing friends leave with armfuls of fragrant plants. The wall will show its full potential over the years, with the twenty rosemary plants forming a supple, oblique line. These take a little longer to establish themselves than herbaceous species, but within a year the lines of the design will become much more obvious.

Once everything was in place, although maintenance is minimal, I knew that the wall needed to be monitored regularly. In the middle of July I suddenly noticed that the felt had dried out. Panic! The plants, which had not yet had time to grow roots in the felt, would not have tolerated a lack of water for more than two days. As it turned out, the batteries of the programmer were flat.

I also very regularly check the mixture of fertilizer and mineral salts, agitated continuously by an aquarium air bubbler to ensure good dissolution. Otherwise, I proceed just as I do for the rest of the garden: deadheading flowers; cutting back foliage when it yellows, so it forms a good tuft again; pruning the subshrubs; keeping an eye on plants that tend to be too invasive; weeding; and remembering to put down slug pellets (Ferramol, an environmentally friendly product) whenever I feel a serious invasion is imminent.

I soon realized that the common sage plants did not want to live like this, whereas all the other sages—including *elegans, dentata, mellifera, syriacum, grahamii,* and hybrids—seemed

The issue of ecology

The green wall is not yet completely "green"! Water consumption is relatively high. The fertilizers, often of chemical origin, are released back into the environment in the case of an open irrigation system; hence the importance of distributing a very dilute solution in which most of the mineral salts will be absorbed by the roots of the plants attached to the wall. Moreover, apart from the irrigation matting, which is made from recycled fabrics, most of the materials used are neither recycled nor recyclable. Fortunately, with new technologies, PVC can now be manufactured with recycled materials.

On the other hand, the dynamism of the wall itself has a definite decontaminating effect, not only from the photosynthesis of the plants but also from the role played by the growing medium. Indeed, the matting acts as a filter for the toxic particles that are retained in it, which are decomposed then mineralized by microorganisms before being absorbed by the plant roots. The more diversity of plant species there is, the better the absorption of all these molecules.

Although this decontaminating effect, combined with the sheer pleasure of being surrounded by greenery, contributes to the well-being of the people living nearby, there is still work to be done if the wall is to become completely environmentally friendly. There are bound to be major developments in this direction in the near future: the plastics industry is evolving rapidly, and PVC manufactured from recycled plastics is already widely available in Japan. Watering times could also be reduced, with the aim of distributing only the amount of water required for wetting the irrigation matting.

particularly happy. This was a pity, because with the purple and variegated varieties of common sage, my wall looked very pretty. I am gradually replacing them as I discover suitable substitutes, at garden centers, nurseries, or plant fairs.

THE PRINCIPLE

The principle is simple: it is just a question of fixing a PVC panel to the wall with wooden battens, covering it with a double layer of irrigation matting, and then inserting the plants. But these plants do not live off thin air: they need watering, and regularly, as there is no earth to retain the water. A rudimentary irrigation system, set along the entire length of the top of the wall, answers this need. A perforated pipe is connected to a pump, activated for a few minutes several times a day—depending on the season and the exposure of the wall—circulates water containing a highly diluted solution of nutrients. Water and nutrients flow down the wall, wetting the

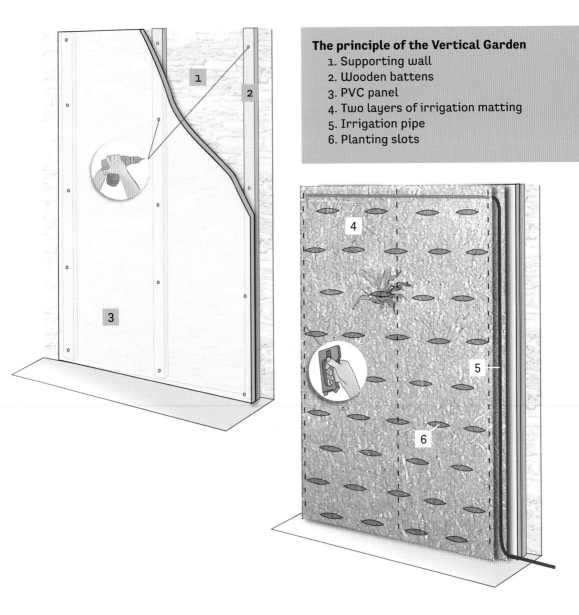

The principle of the Vertical Garden
1. Supporting wall
2. Wooden battens
3. PVC panel
4. Two layers of irrigation matting
5. Irrigation pipe
6. Planting slots

Protection of Patrick Blanc's concept
Patents 8810705, "Apparatus for growing plants without soil on a vertical surface," and 9604526, "Apparatus for growing plants without soil on a substantially vertical surface," protect the unique invention developed by the botanist Patrick Blanc, translated in this book as "vertical garden," the term he adopted in his book *The Vertical Garden* (2008).

Thus, any reproduction, representation, or exploitation of this Vertical Garden (also referred to as a green wall), except for strictly private, noncommercial, and nonpromotional purposes, is subject to Patrick Blanc's prior written consent.

The technical information disclosed in this book relating to the hydroponic process using PVC and irrigation matting should be used exclusively in the context of private enjoyment in a domestic setting.

roots, allowing them to branch out and grow between the fibers of the matting. Once the vertical garden has been built and planted, maintenance must not be neglected: its durability depends on dedicated and regular upkeep.

PLAN YOUR WALL!

Define your project
Don't be afraid to take some time to think and dream. To obtain a result that will meet your expectations, you have to think of all the items you need before you start building. To get an idea of the finished green wall, to imagine how it will integrate, both with the supporting wall and with the style of your garden, don't hesitate to take photos, draw, and lay out the plants on paper, taking their shape and growth into consideration.

After this, consider how irrigation water can be supplied and protected from the elements, examine the condition of the supporting wall, and make sure the future installation will not conflict with neighborhood or co-ownership rules: if the supporting wall is not yours—if it is a party wall or part of a condominium, for instance—make sure that you obtain all the necessary permits before you begin construction.

Also decide on the shape and surface area of your project. Rectangles and squares are the easiest to install and greatly simplify putting the irrigation system into place.

As to the surface area, you can plan for a reasonable width, but it is essential not to exceed a certain height, otherwise there is a risk

The weight of the Vertical Garden per square meter
- Wooden frame: 7–11 lb (3–5 kg), depending on the type of wood
- PVC: 15 lb (7 kg)
- Felt: 7 lb (3 kg)
- Plants: 2–11 lb (1–5 kg)
Total: 3–4 lb per square foot (14–20 kg/m²)

of your wall collapsing. Calculating the load to be borne, and the potential influence of the wind, are essential factors that must be taken into account if the wall is to be more than 7 feet (2 m) tall, and will require the involvement of a professional. Private individuals should moderate their dreams of grandeur! The issue of safety is paramount in this type of structure.

Choosing the right exposure and plants
The ideal is to place your wall so that it is sheltered from wind, hot sun, and frost, all at the same time! A southwestern exposure is perfect. Full sun or extreme shade, as well as frost and

wind, are not the best allies of the vertical garden. The plants should, of course, be chosen according to climate and situation. To adjust frequency of watering to the climate of your area, see page 40. But here are a few tips to counter these risks and to help you deal with extreme situations:

<u>Heat</u>: Too much sunshine will quickly dry out the irrigation matting (felt). Watering frequency should be increased according to how dry the conditions are. In hot, dry conditions, be sure to lower the concentration of fertilizer in the nutrient solution (see pp. 40–43), because evaporation will leave the mineral salts concentrated in the irrigation matting, and will risk burning the roots. In midsummer, at the hottest time of day, don't hesitate to sprinkle the wall with a hose—gently, of course.

<u>Frost</u>: While the branches of plants are protected by buds at their tips, roots have no such natural protection. On irrigation matting, they are particularly vulnerable because they grow "naked" on the support. The felt is quickly taken over by ice, unlike earth, which only freezes on the first few inches of the surface and protects roots from the cold. In regions with cold winters, you should therefore choose very hardy plants, and be sure to shut off irrigation when the temperature drops below the freezing point.

<u>Wind</u>: Avoid exposure to a dominant, continuous wind. The felt will dry out quickly, and drafts will damage fragile foliage.

Plan the work

Forewarned is forearmed! Before starting the work, make things easier for yourself: make a list of the equipment required, plan and submit orders for materials and plants in advance, draw up

---

Some ideal plants for a small Vertical Garden

Plants that enjoy growing on a green wall are those that like having their feet in the shade, as well as those that like well-drained soil, since the water does not stagnate.

Here are some suggestions: oregano, hardy geraniums, *Soleirolia*, lilyturf (*Liriope*), hardy begonias, yellow corydalis (*Corydalis lutea*), fern-leaf corydalis (*Corydalis cheilanthifolia*), white corydalis (*Corydalis ochroleuca*), hostas, astilbes, asters, saxifrages (*Saxifraga fortunei*), *Tellima*, foamflowers (*Tiarella*), western bleeding-heart (*Dicentra formosa*), wild strawberry, *Iris japonica*, *Ophiopogon*, carnations, rock rose.

In addition, the exposure of the plants should not be left to chance. Certainly, the aesthetic side has to be considered (volumes, colors, etc.), but it is essential to meet the needs of the plants, especially in terms of light and heat. Follow these tips:
- To be planted high up, in the sun: sedums, bushy plants, plants that like growing upward (if planted at the bottom, they soon cover up the other plants), etc.
- Lower down, in the shade: ferns, grasses, Eastern teaberry (*Gaultheria procumbens*), etc.
- To be seen from below: alumroot (*Heuchera*), ferns, etc.

LIST OF MATERIALS

Construction of the wall
Support:
- Fully treated pine battens 1.5 in x 2 in (38 mm x 60 mm)
- Panels of microcellular expanded PVC (10 mm thick)
- Polyamide irrigation matting (3 mm thick); allow for 2 layers

Equipment:
- Drill and drill bits suitable for materials to be drilled
- Jigsaw
- Silicone sealant gun
- Electric or pneumatic stapling gun
- Professional-quality utility knife

Hardware:
- Screws, washers, and wall plugs to attach the wooden battens to the supporting wall
- Stainless steel screws and washers to secure the PVC panels
- Mold-resistant silicone sealant
- Roll of 2-inch (5 cm) duct tape (waterproof canvas)
- (10 mm) staples in galvanized steel or, even better, stainless steel

The irrigation system
Support:
- Standard garden watering timer (preferably electronic)
- Fertilizer injector (Dosatron®, for example)
- Basin
- Large container

Equipment:
- Drill and drill bits suitable for materials to be drilled
- Professional-quality utility knife

Hardware:
- Polyurethane tubing, low density, nonporous, ¾ inch (16 or 18 mm)
- Flexible bathroom connector
- 90° elbow fittings, tee fittings, clamps, couplings, end caps, and other fittings as needed

Maintenance
- Aquarium bubbler
- Chemical or organic fertilizers (macronutrients and trace elements)

A well-secured green wall
Pine battens are perfect for small structures like the ones we recommend here for private, individual use. Patrick Blanc's gigantic structures, on the other hand, require a much stronger framework. Nowadays aluminum and galvanized and stainless steel are his materials of choice.

a plan of the support structure, and think about the time needed to do it all. If you are reasonably practical, it takes an average of about two days for a wall of 3 feet by 6½ feet (1 x 2 m), including planting.

MAKING THE WALL

As with any major work, you should avoid trying to take short cuts. The secrets of being a good do-it-yourselfer are to think of every detail in advance and to have all the equipment to hand. There is nothing more annoying than having to leave the job you are doing to rush around different stores looking for something you've forgotten.

STEP 1 / Attaching the wooden battens

The main purpose of the wooden structure is to fix the green wall to the supporting wall, but it has another function as well, less visible but indispensable for ensuring the wall's sustainability. The thickness of the battens ensures that there is a gap of a few inches between the green wall and the supporting wall. This cushion of air provides insulation against cold and heat, and helps to protect the supporting wall from damp.

The garden "eyesore" will soon be no more than an unpleasant memory!

Make a plan for your wall and mark the locations for the holes. Remember to leave space at the top, bottom, and sides to maximize the air cushion effect. Fix the battens vertically, about 1½ ft (0.5 m) apart. Depending on the width chosen for the plant wall, count about four battens for a PVC panel of 3 ft (1.20 m), three battens for 3½ ft (1 m). Mark locations for the holes, following your plan, and then equip yourself with a good

The battens are fastened with screws and washers.

drill and drill bits adapted to the material of the supporting wall. Using wall plugs, screws, and washers, secure each piece of wood every 12 to 18 inches (30–40 cm).

STEP 2 / Installing the PVC panels

The PVC panels are the rigid support for the horticultural felt; they must be installed carefully and completely sealed. Otherwise beware of leaks!

Before fixing the panels in place, make sure you have thought of everything. If the irrigation pipe runs behind the green wall, not above it or to one side, put it in place now; once the PVC is installed, you will no longer have access to it.

Apply the PVC panels so that they rest uniformly flat against the wooden battens. Secure the edges of each panel onto the battens at the edges with stainless steel screws and washers (about ten for a height of 7 feet [2 m]). Then screw the panel, from top to bottom, onto the battens in between. In the case of a large wall requiring multiple PVC panels, connect them by screwing their edges together side by side onto the same batten.

Then seal all screws, joints between panels, and any angles there may be, by applying silicone. Once the silicone dries, seal over it with waterproof duct tape.

STEP 3 / Fastening the irrigation matting

To make it easier to put the plants in place, install a double layer of felt; cutting a small slit in the first layer will allow you to slide the root ball between the two.

Staple the first layer: Start at the top of the wall, leaving a strip of about 6 inches (15 cm) at the top; this will later be wrapped around the irrigation pipe. Staple fairly densely, making sure the matting is pulled perfectly tight. Use the same method to apply the second layer on top of the first.

Three PVC panels are screwed together side by side.

Above: Waterproof duct tape is essential for sealing the joints between the PVC panels and screws.

Right: The irrigation matting is stapled to the PVC panels.

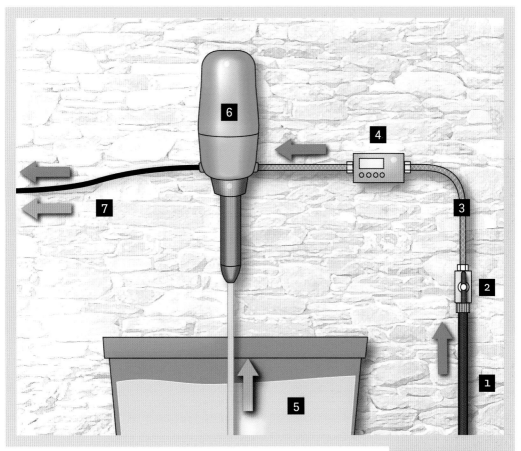

STEP 4 / Installing the irrigation system

No need to call in a plumber if you are a competent do-it-your-selfer. An outside faucet, well sheltered from the elements, is enough to supply irrigation to a wall close by, or even one at a slight distance if there is enough pressure. Leave some space around the faucet, enough room to install the fertilizer injector and a large container. If you are lucky enough to have a garden shed or garage, so much the better! Otherwise, consider building a hut or a large chest of marine plywood close to the wall, with a sloping roof covered with slates or tiles to protect it from the weather.

The "lost water" system is the easiest to put in place. But it is also possible to install, against the bottom of the wall, a water recovery tank fitted with a submersible pump. But let us look at the first system: a fertilizer injector pumps nutrient into water from the domestic supply, under pressure. The resulting solution is then routed to the perforated irrigation pipe positioned along the top of the wall. A timer controls the frequency of irrigation.

Fit a valve to the inlet from the water supply. Fix the electronic timer and the fertilizer injector to the wall, and install them according to their respective instruction manuals. Place a large container under the injector. With a flexible connector hose, connect the water supply to the programmer and the programmer to the injector. Connect one

The strip of surplus irrigation matting is wrapped around the perforated irrigation pipe and stapled into place.

end of the polyurethane hose to the injector and get ready to connect the perforated irrigation pipe to the other end. Depending on the configuration of your installation, make sure you have all the hardware you will need: elbow fittings, tee fittings, clamps, sleeves, couplings, etc.

Now is also the time to think about protecting the installation and the circuit against freezing.

STEP 5 / Connecting the irrigation pipe

For small areas, so long as the irrigation pipe is positioned horizontally, it is not worth equipping it with special drippers. Small, well-placed holes are sufficient, and will save both time and money.

With a 2 mm (size 47) drill bit, drill holes every 4 inches (10 cm) in the polyurethane tube. Connect it to the irrigation system and position it at the top of the wall with the holes pointing downward, against the strip of surplus felt that was previously left over. Seal both ends of the pipe with plugs and then fix it to the wall, wrapping the strip of irrigation matting around it and stapling directly below the pipe to hold it firmly in place. This arrangement has many advantages: it keeps the pipe in place, it looks good, it helps protect against freezing, and it ensures good water diffusion.

STEP 6 / Setting the water flow and final adjustments

This is the last step before planting. Do not neglect it, even if you are burning with desire to start putting the plants into your vertical garden. Precise adjustment of the water flow will ensure a healthy, sustainable wall. Always under pressure (usually 3 bars), the water supply flowing into our homes can climb to the topmost floors, and, here, reach our perforated irrigation pipe.

Give the irrigation water a "dry run"
Before planting, if you have the opportunity, run the daily irrigation cycles and wait for a few weeks. Bacteria will proliferate, the irrigation matting will become impregnated with the nutrient solution and mosses will invade the wall. Perfect conditions for planting!

Start the program and watch how the water flows out of the irrigation pipe. Take care not to burst the pipe; it is best to start slowly, gradually opening the faucet more widely, continuously monitoring what happens. See if water is flowing out of each hole for good flow distribution and check that there is no leakage. Observe the humidification of the felt: it should be uniformly wet, right down to the bottom. If this is not so, do not hesitate to drill more holes above areas that are too dry. After some experimentation, you will find the ideal rate of flow.

Set the timer, depending on the frequency and duration of the irrigation cycles, set the injector, and adjust the dosage of fertilizer (see pp. 40–43).

A wall in a closed circuit.

Alternative: a circuit with water recovery

In this alternative option, the fertilizer injector is replaced by a tank that recovers the drainage water and a small submersible pump that propels the water back, to operate in a closed circuit. You can choose between adding dissolved nutrients to the tank, or you can install a pond, where natural organic material—aquatic plants, fish excrement, dead insects, and microscopic algae—will provide the necessary nutrients; this would be a more ecological solution. Note that unless this pond is directly fed by its own water supply, you will need to keep an eye on the water level and top it up when necessary.

If you choose this option, you will need to modify the plan for the wall slightly, because it cannot descend right down to the ground; you must allow room for the recovery tank at the foot of the wall. A wall of 7 feet x 4 feet (2 m x 1 m) will need a tank of 53 US gallons (200 L). Camouflage the tank, boxing it in with marine plywood, for example. If you have room, you could situate the tank in a more distant location, linking it to a gutter that collects drainage water—a good challenge for the do-it-yourselfer!

STEP 7 / Planting

After all the hard work of installing the wall, here at last is the fun part! You still need to be well organized, though. The plants should all be at hand and in good condition, because they will be living on their reserves during their first weeks on the wall.

Draw up the plan of the plants' location on a sheet of paper, taking account of their shapes, their colors, and how they grow. Draw the locations of the different plants onto the irrigation matting with chalk, following the plan. Using a utility knife, make horizontal incisions of 4 inches (10 cm) in the outer layer of felt. Cut very carefully, to avoid damaging the second layer of felt. Gently remove a maximum amount of soil from around the roots of each plant. Install plants in different slots. Tamp gently around the roots, and then staple around the root ball so that it is held properly in place.

Draw the design with chalk, and then cut the slots with a utility knife in the first layer of felt, always in staggered rows. After removing the soil from around the roots, position each plant in its slot, and then staple around the root ball to fix it in place.

Other techniques for growing green walls without soil

There are alternatives to Patrick Blanc's technique; some present certain advantages, but , as always, the question of durability is paramount.

Changing the support of the green wall: Instead of using PVC panels, polypropylene sheeting is fixed to panels of marine plywood using neoprene adhesive. Although more affordable, this type of support will resist weather conditions and constant watering for only a few years.

Changing the growing medium: A rigid mesh is used to secure a layer of hydrophilic porous material, about 4 inches (10 cm) thick, onto a wall in sealed marine plywood. Blocks of peat moss, horticultural rock wool, perlite, vermiculite, pozzolana, or coir are perfectly suited to this type of wall. This type of vertical garden gives the plants better resistance to freezing conditions because the substrate is thicker than irrigation matting, and therefore protects the roots better. However, it is difficult to assess the durability of such walls; porous materials of this kind can quickly start to become compacted, and if this happens the root fibers can break and the plants will die.

The wall of aromatic plants in late November, when the plants begin to go dormant. As in conventional gardens, some plants lose their leaves in winter while others keep them, but here the mosses growing on the felt keep it always looking green.

UPKEEP AND GOOD HEALTH OF THE WALL

A green wall takes very little time to maintain, but it requires careful and regular monitoring. If you are going away for several weeks, leave your keys with a neighbor: disaster can ensue if, for instance, the programmer stops working because of dead batteries and no one is around to do anything about it.

IRRIGATION

It is impossible to give hard-and-fast advice about irrigation. Everything depends on exposure, on the climate of your area, and on the plants selected. It is therefore necessary to test and observe carefully in order to find the ideal cycles, without forgetting to adjust for each change of season and during particular weather conditions.

After each sequence of irrigation, the felt should be uniformly wet, and should still be slightly damp just before the following sequence. Be sure to choose an electronic program that can be precisely adapted to the watering frequency you have selected.

At night, in winter, and during long periods of rain, reduce the frequency of irrigation.

During periods of hot weather or strong sunlight, the frequency and duration should be increased.

In frosty weather, the most reasonable solution is to reduce or stop irrigation: plants can bear a few days' fasting in winter, whereas continuing to irrigate could damage the circuit, the felt, and the roots of plants whose cells might burst. If freezing conditions continue, shut off the water supply completely and drain the circuit.

Here is a rough estimate on which to base your tests:
Frequency: 3–6 times per day.
Duration: Between one and five minutes, depending on water pressure and distribution on the felt.
It will be up to you to find the right ratio between frequency and duration.

NUTRIENTS

Nutrients are essential for plant growth. But in soilless culture on an inert support, such as irrigation matting, there is no natural nutrient intake, with the exception of large organic molecules (for instance VOCs, or volatile organic compounds, such as formaldehyde), which are broken down by the microbes growing on the irrigation matting, converted into smaller molecules, and absorbed by plant roots. That is why it is necessary to feed the plants by adding nutrients to the water. During irrigation, the injector consistently releases fertilizer containing macro- and micronutrients that plants assimilate immediately. Do not get discouraged, even if the procedure for finding the correct dosage of fertilizer seems tedious: it must be perfectly mastered. So do not skip this step and regularly check the state of the nutrient solution. The solution used is very dilute indeed: between 0.007 and 0.014 ounces per liter (0.2–0.4 gm/L), which is about ten times less than is commonly used in horticulture and agriculture.

Choosing the right fertilizer

Nutrients are composed of minerals. They are classified into two categories:

- Macronutrients: Plants need large quantities. Most common fertilizers contain the essential trio of nitrogen, phosphorus, and potassium, but some also contain secondary elements (calcium, sulfur, magnesium), and it is worth choosing these.
- Trace elements (micronutrients), too, are indispensable, but in smaller quantities.

In the container

The nutrients are diluted in the water tank located under the fertilizer injector. If you have room, choose a large-capacity tank; setting up new dosages and checking the concentration will not have to be done so frequently.

A reserve of 50 liters of solution can last for two months or so. But don't let that stop you from checking every week, because everything depends on the programming, the flow, the pres-

Moderately hard water

Hard water affects the absorption of nutrients by the roots. We must, in this case, increase the amount of fertilizer. The utility that supplies the domestic water in your area can inform you about water hardness.

Here are the recommended dosages for the nutrient solution:

WATER HARDNESS	QUANTITY OF MACRONUTRIENTS per liter of irrigation water	QUANTITY OF TRACE ELEMENTS per liter of irrigation water
Soft water (mineral concentration 0–60 mg/L)	0.20 g	0.10 ml
Moderately hard water (mineral concentration 61–120 mg/L)	0.30 g	0.15 ml
Hard to very hard water (mineral concentration 121 mg/L and over)	0.40 g	0.20 ml

sure, and the season. A small aquarium bubbler placed in the tank will ensure that the solution is well mixed. Otherwise, stir it regularly.

Nutrient dosage for a closed circuit
Dosage must be reduced: in fact, debris from plants, insects, and other sources will enrich the recovered and recycled water. And if the tank contains fish, their leftover food and excrement will enrich the water naturally to the point that it may be possible to completely avoid using fertilizer.

The operation of the fertilizer injector
The injector is used to regulate the amount of nutrient solution to be mixed with the irrigation water. The higher the setting, the higher the concentration of nutrient in the water: if the injector is set at 0.2%, it will dissolve 1 liter of nutrient in 500 liters of water, but if you set it to 2%, it will dissolve 1 liter in only 50 liters of water. We must therefore make sure to adjust the amount of fertilizer in the tank correctly, by carefully regulating the injector (see box below). The ideal is to set the injector to 0.2%, but you can increase the percentage during periods of rapid growth, when you water the plants more, if the plants are showing signs of deficiency.

Varying the dosages
Remember to adjust your dosages according to the climate; plants do not have the same nutritional needs everywhere. During hot weather, evaporation of water creates a higher concentration of minerals in the irrigation matting, and thus the amount of fertilizer must be reduced.

In winter, plants photosynthesize less, their growth slows down, and consequently they need less food. In this case, too, you need to lower their nutrient intake.

Preparing the nutrient solution
To determine the amount of macronutrients and micronutrients to put in the reserve tank, you can perform this simple calculation:

> **Amount of macro- and micronutrients, depending on water hardness**
> **X**
> **Liters of irrigation water**

Example: If your injector is set at 0.2%, or 1 liter of nutrient solution mixed with 500 liters of domestic water, for moderately hard water you will have:
- 0.3 g of macronutrients x 500 liters of irrigation water = 150 g of macronutrients per liter of water in the tank.
- 0.15 ml of trace elements x 500 liters = 75 ml of trace elements per liter of water in the tank.

MAINTAINING THE HEALTH OF THE WALL

You may find the wall's appearance surprising at first. The roots cannot penetrate the growing medium, so they grow on the surface. Mosses, molds, and fungi invade the wall and mingle with the roots growing on the felt in a tangled white and green mass. Do not worry: this is normal, and it helps to keep the wall healthy. There is no need to worry either if some plants die: plants are living things, and may sometimes perish for no apparent reason.

There are, however, some signs you should pay attention to if they become widespread. Here are some common problems:

Wilting leaves

Probable explanation: the growing medium is too dry and the plants are thirsty. Simply increase the frequency of irrigation.

If this situation occurs in summer and the growing medium is wet, it means that the plants are too hot. Spray them with water at night with a sprinkler. In regions where the summers are very hot, plant heat-resistant species.

Discolored leaves

Discoloration that is more pronounced toward the middle of the leaves is a sign of excessive watering; reduce the watering duration. Leaves that are discolored but have green veins indicate iron deficiency due to hard water. To fight against iron chlorosis, put a special anti-chlorosis product into the tank, or increase the dosage of the nutrient solution to compensate for the hardness of the water.

Uniform discoloration indicates a generalized and widespread deficiency, and probably means that you should increase the dosage of the nutrient solution, or that it is time to renew it.

Discoloration of the edges of the leaves, or stripes, is a sign of calcium deficiency; calcium should be added to the nutrient solution.

The vertical garden: a major consumer of water?

With a vertical garden, there is no water retention, as there is in the soil. Water consumption thus is relatively high, especially in a lost water irrigation system; if you irrigate for three minutes five times a day with a partially open faucet, this uses up the same amount of water as a person taking a shower.

Moreover, the wall has to be watered throughout the year, while you only have to water a conventional garden in summer, and then only when plants have recently been installed. On the other hand, with a green wall there is no loss from water percolating through the soil, as is the case with a garden.

Here are two tips for combining reduced consumption with aesthetic interest:

- Plant a few perennials at the foot of the wall; they will be happy to consume the surplus water.

- In an open or a closed circuit, install a pond filled with plants and/or fish. There is no need to worry about the health of the fish so long as the nutrient solution is at a very low dose.

Wherever possible, use recycled rainwater for irrigation.

OTHER TECHNIQUES

Although the classic method is still to put plants directly into the earth and then to train them upward as climbers or as espaliers depending on the way they grow, there is also no shortage of tricks for gardeners to hang flowerpots and planters on walls in various ways. Here are a variety of ideas for decorating different kinds of vertical surfaces with living plants.

GROWING CLIMBERS AND TRELLIS PLANTS

Climbers soften and mellow stern-looking facades, twining around pillars and perfuming patios. They give relief to gardens, softly embroidering them to reflect their owners' personal taste, and help to integrate buildings and other structures into the garden. But they are not the only plants able to decorate walls. Many ornamental and fruit trees are suitable as espaliers, provided their growth is not too vigorous and is easily controllable.

CLIMBING PLANTS

Fixing methods

Although they are unable to stand erect, climbing plants are very clever, and they do not hesitate to exploit their neighbors, crawling and creeping through them and clinging to them in their quest for the essential light they need to flourish. Whether they are woody or herbaceous, if they have no support, they crawl along the ground until they find a branch or pole, which they then take over as fast as they can.

Each climber has its own way of sending out flexible branches to cling to its support. Some twining plants climb the host plant by wrapping their stems around it in a spiral, always turning in the same direction (clockwise or counterclockwise; this is what differentiates, for example, Chinese from Japanese wisteria). Others cling on with strong tendrils, as with vines. In the clematis, it is the petiole that wraps around a thin branch or a wire. Virginia creepers adhere to their support with adhesive pads, while ivy clings on with aerial roots, forming crampons that are almost impossible to tear off.

Before buying a climber to decorate a column or to hide a wall, it is therefore essential to know its mode of attachment. There is, indeed, a climber suitable for each kind of support: column, pillar, gazebo, pergola, wall, wooden or wire fence, tree, or shrub. On a wall, choose plants with crampons or adhesive pads. Twining plants are perfect for a trellis. Plants with tendrils establish themselves quickly on wires and fences. If you plant a woody climber, remember to take into account how big it will grow when mature.

Not all climbers, however, are able to cling on completely by themselves. Lengths of twine, raffia, reinforced plastic, plastic-coated wire, or specially designed ties must be used to attach these plants to their supports; you therefore need to keep an eye on them, as wear and tear due to weather and other conditions can very often get the better of the ties.

The winter, after the leaves have fallen, is a good time to check the strength and general condition of the ties, and to replace or consolidate them where necessary. Take the opportunity to fix the branches that have grown during the fall. Install hooks on masonry walls, and on timber supports use fasteners with a nail and a plastic loop. Be careful not to over-tighten the ties, so as not to injure the stems.

Pay attention to your roof

If climbers generally do no harm to walls—on the contrary, they serve as insulation—it is not the same for roofs. Check regularly that stems are not creeping in between your roof tiles or slates.

How to plant

<u>In the ground</u>: Pay attention to soil and exposure. Dig a hole 2 feet (0.5 m) in all directions, add compost, and put the plant in place. Fill in the hole, and then water thoroughly. Continue to water from May to October during the year following planting. Guide the plant up the support as it grows. If you are sowing seeds of annual climbers, dig over and weed the ground first. These annuals can decorate all kinds of supports by themselves, or they can be trained to cling to woody climbers, brightening them up in summer.

<u>In pots</u>: To decorate the facings of terraces or to twine around balcony railings, it is possible to grow climbers in tubs

1. To plant a potted cup-and-saucer vine (Cathedral Bells; *Cobaea scandens*), make a big hole, two to three times the size of the root ball in all directions.
2. Mix compost into the soil. Position the plant then fill in.
3. Guide the plant toward its support, keeping the original stakes at first.
4. Spread out the branches and tie them with raffia.
5. Water without wetting the foliage.

and troughs if you follow a few basic principles. Whether it is made of wood, terracotta, cement, or stone, the container must be at least 2 feet (0.5 m) in diameter for a woody plant, and from 8 to 12 inches (20 to 30 cm) for annuals. Prepare growing medium composed of ⅔ potting soil and ⅓ garden soil, adding a handful of organic compost. Check that the drain holes are present and functioning, and then place a 3 to 4 inch (7–10 cm) layer of clay pellets in the bottom to ensure good drainage. Watering is indispensable when planting, but afterward will depend on the weather. Generally, the soil should have dried out between two waterings. A good surface treatment, applied each year in March to a depth of 4 inches (10 cm), with a mixture of potting soil and compost, will keep the container in good condition.

Ideal climbing plants

<u>Annuals</u>: Annual climbers are charming, fast-growing, and free-flowering. When you plant them in May, they put on a show all summer long, overflowing their pots, twining around hanging baskets, covering over fences, mingling with each other.

Annual climbers are easy to sow, grow faster and, above all, flower for longer than most perennials, with which they also elegantly intertwine. Use them to decorate an old grille or a wooden fence; let them climb up a spring-flowering shrub and see it bloom twice in the year; or sow them at the foot of a facade with a trellis.

Ideal for brightening up a wall, they will cling to any support, lighting up forgotten corners. They have their place on the balcony, where they love to twine around railings and even windowsills. You can always find the opportunity to grow one up a tree trunk, to slip another one into a pottery container so that it trails down prettily. They include *Ipomoea* (or morning glory), cup-and-saucer vine (*Cobaea scandens*), sweet peas, nasturtiums, and others.

A garland of morning glory greets the visitor.

Opposite: A fine example of trellising: *Pyracantha* 'Soleil d'Or' flowering in spring. In autumn and winter it is covered with shiny golden-yellow berries.

<u>Woody climbers</u>:

Plants with crampons, aerial roots that fix them firmly to their support, whether a wall or the bark of a tree. These plants do not need outside help because they have a powerful grip and cling to almost any surface. Among them are ivy, climbing hydrangea, *Schizophragma*, trumpet vine (*Campsis radicans*), and *Pileostegia*.

- Plants with adhesive pads or suction cups: For large surfaces such as gables of houses, these plants are perfect because they do not need help to cling on. Virginia creepers: *Parthenocissus quiquefolia*, *Parthenocissus henryana*, *Parthe-*

The hop 'Prima Donna' tangles itself around a wooden trellis.

nocissus tricuspidata (Boston ivy), and others.

- Plants with tendrils (such as vines, clematis, sweet peas, passion flowers, *Cobaea*): The tendrils are modified leaflets or petioles, which some plants use to raise themselves up and then to cling to trellises, fences, teepees, shrubs, or trees.

- Plants with twining stems that curl around their support (trellises and other openwork, arches, trees, etc.): Wisteria, honeysuckle, hops, jasmine, birthwort (*Aristolochia*), *Akebia*, jasmine nightshade (*Solanum jasminoides*), *Trachelospermum*, perennial or annual morning glory (*Ipomoea*).

- Thorny plants: Roses and brambles use their thorns to hang on and climb up into trees or on trellises, arches, and pergolas. You need to keep a regular eye on these plants to make sure they do not detach themselves.

TRELLIS PLANTS

Why attach plants to a trellis?

The long arching branches of some plants are unable to stand up straight, as they are not woody enough, but at the same time they are not capable of attaching themselves to a support. This is the case with winter jasmine; to grow best, it needs to be fastened to a support. A system for firmly attaching the plant, with metal wire attached to studs, holds the branches securely in place. All you have to do then is to train them as they grow.

Other plants may be grown in this way even if their branches are not flexible or twining, but it requires a lot of hard pruning work. This method is based on the cultivation of espalier fruit trees.

The more limited the space available, the more useful are espalier shrubs, because they can be coiled into the smallest corners, leaning against existing supports such as walls, trellises, and fences. Their form will give a lot of personality to the garden. Walls are a good protection against cold winds for plants in general, and you can grow trellis plants against them that would be too delicate to grow elsewhere. They will bear flowers and fruit more quickly.

How to espalier

You need to guide branches from an early age, when they are still supple, onto stretched metal wires, trellises, or lattices. This is not difficult, but it requires patience. The support must be strong enough to cope with the shrub becoming heavier as it grows over the years.

The branches are tied loosely with metal clamps padded with foam plastic so as not to injure the bark. Branches must be able to grow without being strangled. All you need to do is to attach the young shoots you want to keep as they grow, and to remove unwanted ones with secateurs.

To enhance both flowering and fruiting, stems are forced out horizontally while they are still flexible. This disturbs the circulation of the sap, which cannot rise directly to the ends of the branches; the production of flowers and fruit thus increases significantly.

To limit their growth and to keep them looking elegant, these plants should be pruned every year in March, when they start to grow, in June, and again in September, just before they become dormant.

Ideal espalier plants

A living sculpture or a nice warm coat—espaliered plants can play all kinds of roles. Almost all fruit trees can be grown in this way. In Normandy, the gables of many houses are taken over by large, carefully trained pear trees. Espaliers grown as palmettes or fans, and cordons, can look very impressive, whether grown along walls or as a free-standing barrier to define the limits of a vegetable garden.

Here is a small selection of ornamental plants that can be grown in this way to obtain a guaranteed effect: evergreen *Ceanothus,* cotoneaster, *Pyracantha,* camellias, buddleia, *Weigela,* flannel bush (*Fremontodendron*), and Japanese quince (*Chaenomeles*).

Apple trees grown as a palmette, in a single or double U shape, are a superb "living fence" for a vegetable garden at the Delbard nurseries in Malicorne, France.

DO-IT-YOURSELF

Often, being patient is more important than being an outstanding do-it-yourselfer when making these compositions, which are alternatives to walls of climbing plants or vertical gardens. But, after all, isn't patience the gardener's prime quality?

Plants:
Different succulent plants, such as sedums, sempervivums, and saxifrages.
Materials:
Terracotta flower pots
System for attaching the pots to the wall
Potting soil and sand, or special potting soil for succulents

MAKING YOUR OWN WALL OF TERRACOTTA POTS

Here is a cheap method, both for do-it-yourselfers and for those with creative minds. The wall of clay pots is a good alternative to the hydroponic technique and is a very appealing idea for gardeners who feel hesitant about getting involved in a complex and costly system. As it makes use of a traditional growing medium, the supply of water and nutrient solution is the same as for window boxes.

The idea is to create a vertical space where clay pots are placed very close together to give the visual effect of a wall of plants. All you have to do is let your imagination run free, and you can get results that are very personal and original, and often surprising.

For example, opt for a wall of small, old flower pots (easy to find at garage sales) in which you can grow a collection of rock plants. Or have fun hanging up different sizes and shapes of pots, arranging them in a curve. Play around with their rounded shapes to create a real abstract design, paying attention to how you position the pots, and to the growing habits of the plants themselves.

Watering the wall can be approached in two ways: a small watering can with a long spout is the simplest, especially for plants that require little water—rockery plants such as saxifrages, sempervivums, or sedums. For more demanding plants, consider borrowing from the concept of hydroponic walls by installing, above the pots, small pipes pierced with holes, connected to a larger one, with a timer to set off watering at appropriate times.

Step 1 / Before you start, consider the weight: the clay pot and the soil, combined with the irrigation water, can be very heavy. Do not neglect this aspect: choose suitable fastening systems.

Step 2 / Create the basic structure. It must be firmly fixed to the wall to support the weight of the pots and their contents. Several types of materials are suitable: buy or scavenge rigid

The aesthetic aspect
You should think about the aesthetics of the support structure and also of the clay pots themselves. If your pots are old
and weathered, it is best to leave them as they are. But you
can decorate new pots by painting them with outdoor house
paint or—more ecologically friendly—with lime paint. Paint
them however you like, using natural pigments; with a plain
color if you want them to melt into the background, or with
a colored pattern if you want them to stand out. You can also
make pretty pot covers out of canvas made of vegetable fiber
(such as flax or hemp) to give a country feel to your wall.
Remember that the choice of a wall of flowerpots implies
relatively small containers, and thus reduced plant growth,
because root development is limited to the size of the pot.

wire mesh, metal or wooden trellis, interwoven metal strips,
or other supports. The important thing is to have a support
that is firmly harnessed to the wall, so that neither the wind
nor the weight of the pots can move it.

Step 3 / Once this structure is solidly anchored, you can leave
it as it is or dress it up with wicker fencing or canvas made
from plant fibers such as flax, jute, or hemp. In any case the
structure, whether dressed up or not, must look discreet.

Step 4 / Finally, all that remains for you to do is to devise a
system of hooks for the terracotta pots. For example, you can
thread a thick wire through the hole at the bottom of the pot
and shape it into a hook at the top to secure it to the support.
Be careful not to block up the hole completely, as water must
still be able to flow through it.

MAKING SHELVES FOR PLANTS

Draw up a clear plan before you begin.
The size of the structure depends on
what you want and where it is located,
but if it takes up an entire wall, it will
look wonderful!

Build a kind of backless bookcase, with
compartments of different sizes, just as
you would do for books. Make sure you
make it strong enough, because the pots
and wet soil can be quite heavy. The wood
must be thoroughly treated and sealed
so it will resist weather and spills from
watering. It could be painted to match
your garden furniture or the dominant
tone of garden flowers. Drill several
holes to fasten your "bookcase" securely
to the wall.

Plants:
Outdoor ferns, as many as you like, in dif-
ferent sizes
Materials:
- A jigsaw, or, even better, a circular saw,
and a drill (to drill holes to attach the
shelves to the wall)
- A level
- Sheets of marine plywood or recycled
shelves
- Terracotta flowerpots of different sizes
- Saucers to go under the flowerpots
- Clay pellets
- Leaf mold

Some of the compartments can measure up to 28 inches (70 cm) square, others only 8 inches (20 cm); it is the mixture of different sizes that will give the composition its charm.

If you are not particularly good with your hands, explore flea markets and yard sales, where you'll find indoor furniture designed to hold television sets, books, and other objects, or old bookcases with different-sized compartments. Make sure the piece you have set your heart on is strong enough for the purpose. All that remains for you to do then is to treat, seal, and paint it (see pp. 94–97).

DESIGNING AN EPHEMERAL CIRCLE

Materials:
- A round container 2 to 3 inches (5–7 cm) deep, and about 12 inches (30 cm) in diameter, in a lightweight material such as zinc, aluminum, or stainless steel
- A drill with a fine bit, or a gimlet, depending on the material of the container
- Chicken wire
- Clay pellets
- Soil
- Wood moss
- Galvanized wire

This little floral composition is very simple to make: a round container, serving as a frame, is filled with clay pellets and soil held in place by a fine mesh.

The soil, in this position, will begin to settle and mass together after a period of some weeks. When the plants start to become unstable, do not hesitate to dig them up and replant them in the garden or a more conventional container. Put your frame away until next season, or use it again right away to create a whole new composition.

You can rejuvenate your frame by painting it. In the same spirit, you could make a square or rectangular window, for example by recycling old canteen trays.

Step 1 / Drill eight holes ½ inch (1 cm) from the edge: two at the top, 1 inch (2 cm) apart, and the other six at 2 o'clock, 3 o'clock, 5 o'clock, 7 o'clock, 9 o'clock, and 10 o'clock. Insert a wire through the top two holes; this will be used to hang the composition on the wall.

Step 2 / Place the chicken wire over the top of the container. Wearing protective gloves, and using a wire cutter, cut it out, leaving a margin of about 1 inch (2 cm) around the outside; this margin should be untwisted. Solidify the whole assembly by twisting it together again, using six lengths of galvanized wire, to go through the six holes you drilled earlier. Fold the lengths of wire to create a "table" with the same dimensions as the container, into which it will fit.

Step 3 / With the container placed flat, poke each "table leg" into

Three cheers for clay pellets!
Clay pellets weigh almost nothing, so they lighten the growing medium and reduce its tendency to settle and mass together. And they do not interfere with the roots of the plants, which grow in between the pellets.

its hole, still leaving access to the inside of the container. Fill the container with growing medium: clay pellets and soil, with wood moss on top, to within ½ inch (1 cm) of the top.

Step 4 / Lift up the container, gently pressing the mesh until it is resting on the moss. Mind your hands when the wires come out through the back. If necessary, rework the edges a bit so that the mesh perfectly covers the soil. Finally, delicately pull the wires from behind; the growing medium must be well secured but not crushed. Twist the wires together to seal the cage: 9 o'clock with 3 o'clock, 10 o'clock with 5 o'clock, and 2 o'clock with 7 o'clock.

Step 5 / To plant, make a hole in the wire mesh for each plant; remove the excess moss and install the plant.

A circular composition with three different sempervivums.

READY-TO-INSTALL VERTICAL GARDENS

If you do not want to make your life complicated but still want to be creative by putting plants on the walls around you, there are more and more companies offering fast and convenient solutions for making your world green. With the smaller installations, you are not risking much, but you need to be careful with larger structures.

PLANTING ON WALLS IS TRENDY!

Patrick Blanc has achieved worldwide fame with his creations, and they have inspired "vocations" in a whole lot of other people! Various companies have jumped on the bandwagon, and vertical planting has turned into a commercial bonanza.

But mastery of these complex systems for planting without soil requires long experience and extensive knowledge. Indeed, it is necessary not only to perfect a fully developed, durable technique (remember that Patrick Blanc's concept is protected by a patent), but also to posses a complete knowledge of plant physiology. Thus, many manufacturers come and go with the seasons, and it is not easy to find your way around.

There are two kinds of proposals for prefabricated vertical gardens:

- Some companies will install large-scale vertical gardens at the homes of private individuals, using different hydroponic techniques.

- Small vertical compositions for you to plant yourself are sold in garden centers and online. Some are suitable for growing outside and are not already planted, which allows you to give free rein to your creative ideas.

Defy gravity!
Vertical gardens have to be light in weight if they are to last. The heavier the growing medium, the more it will clump together and settle down over time; the upper parts will die. Some significant figures: wet horticultural felt 3 mm thick weighs about 7 pounds per square foot (3 kg/m²) while common 1 inch (2 cm) growing mediums reach 44 pounds (20 kg), and those of 4 inches (10 cm), 220 pounds (100 kg)!

PROFESSIONALLY INSTALLED VERTICAL GARDENS

Most companies have registered their systems, which typically consist of small modules of galvanized steel, stacked on one another, filled with growing medium based on sphagnum moss, rock wool, or coir.

Every wall is a unique project, developed with the client. Once the estimate has been approved, technicians come to install the wall in the home. Some professionals also offer a maintenance contract.

Whatever your choice, think carefully about your project,

check the extent of the guarantee, and ask to see designs that have already been completed.

Some sources for reference: Casaverde®; WALLFLORE® by PlantOver; Végétalis® by Greenwall; Canevaflor® (see pp. 141–42 for contact information).

PLANT PICTURES

Accroplant

The Accroplant in the photo is a "plant picture" with a very stylish look, containing an internal irrigation system and five small "balconies" filled with a soil-based growing medium in which to grow your favorite plants. The company, which is no longer in business, produced two models for outside use, one in brushed aluminum, the other in carbon. Dimensions: 28 inches (70 cm) long, 19 inches (48 cm) high, 3 inches (7 cm) deep. A similar system is currently available from Dorian Green, a company that specializes in indoor ready-made plant pictures but also sells empty 12-inch (30 cm) square frames in a zinc finish, filled with growing medium, for you to plant yourself.

Order from www.doriangreen.fr.

Le P'tit mur végétal, by Idées B Création

Very simple, these bags made of black polypropylene fabric are fitted with large pockets to contain the soil. They just have to be sprinkled with a watering can with a long spout. As the black plastic does not look particularly nice, you need to choose the right sort of plants, so they will hide it completely.

There are two formats:

- four-pocket format: 43 inches (109 cm) high, 14 inches (35 cm) long; pockets: 10 inches (25 cm) high, 10 inches (25 cm) long.

- twelve-pocket format: 31 inches (80 cm) high, 39 inches (100 cm) long; pockets: 10 inches (25 cm) high, 10 inches (25 cm) long.

Order from www.webtrouvailles.fr.

Top: A ready-made composition by Accroplant.

Bottom: An outside vertical garden by Wallflore on a terrace in Paris.

Sphagnum moss: an ecological growing medium?
The accumulation of organic matter in this moss is responsible for the formation of peat bogs. The moss that is now sold in France comes from the island of Chiloé in Chile. It is presented by its importers as THE ecologically friendly growing medium, as it is produced in a sustainable way: harvested every four years to ensure its renewal. It is also supposed to consume very little water.

The problem is, however, that its renewal is counted in decades rather than years. Thus, harvesting sphagnum moss induces the destruction of peat bogs and of an entire ecosystem. It is no coincidence that it is imported from Chile, even though there is no lack of peat bogs in Europe; European peat bogs are protected by strict regulations.

COMPOSITIONS

FOLLOWING THE VERTICAL GARDEN CONCEPT

Here are some ideas you can put into practice to "copy," on a reduced scale, the concept of the vertical garden. Keep in mind that, to avoid the risk of accidents, these structures must not exceed 7 feet (2 m) in height. For larger sizes you should consult a professional. And don't forget that they can be installed only for personal use.

FOLIAGE WALL

Plants (perennials)
- 10 reed canary grass, *Phalaris arundinacea* 'Feesey'
- 6 cogon grass (Japanese blood grass). *Imperata cylindrica* 'Red Baron'
- 6 *Hosta* 'Honeybells'
- 5 coral bells, *Heuchera* 'Black Beauty'
- 5 coral bells, *Heuchera* 'Citronelle'
- 5 hairy alumroot, *Heuchera villosa* 'Chantilly'
- 9 lamb's ear, *Stachys byzantina* 'Silver Carpet'
- 5 bugle, *Ajuga reptans* 'Burgundy Glow'
- 5 bugle, *Ajuga reptans* 'Atropurpurea'
- 15 silver mound, *Artemisia schmidtiana* 'Nana'
- 3 curry plant, *Helichrysum italicum* ssp. *serotinum*
- 6 black mondo grass, *Ophiopogon planiscapus* 'Nigrescens'
- 9 common rue, *Ruta graveolens* 'Jackman's Blue'

PREPARATION TIME:
STRUCTURE: 2 DAYS
PLANTING: 8 HOURS

VERTICAL GARDEN CONCEPT
Surface: A wall 7 feet (2 m) wide by 7 feet (2 m) high.
Planting: In pockets.
Maintenance: Watering, controlled by a programmer, delivering diluted fertilizer through perforated pipes from the top of the wall.

SELECTED PLANTS
- *Phalaris arundinacea* (reed canary grass): The variety 'Feesey' is much less invasive than the species plant. This grass grows with long, light blades, creamy white with hints of pink, edged and streaked with bright green. The slender, erect flowering stems, 4 feet (1.2 m) to 5 feet (1.5 m) high, are pale green with purple tints.
    - *Imperata cylindrica* 'Red Baron' (cogon grass) is an absolutely ravishing grass: Everybody loves its red and fluorescent bright green foliage.
    - *Hosta* 'Honeybells.' The light plays with the bright green foliage of this hosta. It has pretty mauve flowers.
    - The *Heuchera,* with their evergreen rosettes, have stunning colors: purple, almost black, lemon, and silver. They bloom in thin spikes.
    - The cultivar *Stachys byzantina* 'Silver Carpet' (lamb's ear) does not flower, but its furry silver evergreen foliage blends with the support.
    - Ajugas (bugle) are of creeping habit, and adhere well to the support. The foliage of 'Burgundy Glow' is variegated purple, pink, green, and cream. The leaves of 'Atropurpurea' are purple and very glossy. Both have blue flowers and evergreen leaves.
    - For a fine carpet of silver, nothing beats *Artemisia schmidtiana* 'Nana' (silver mound).
    - The long thin silver evergreen leaves of *Helichrysum italicum* ssp. *serotinum* (curry plant) are particularly famous for their scent of curry.
    - Maybe the blackest plant it is possible

Heart-shaped, ribbed, frayed, pleated . . . tender green, bright green, dark green, ivory, purple, violet, gold, lemon, blue, pink . . . soft, velvety, furry, felt-like, woolly, shiny . . . the diversity of foliage is endless!

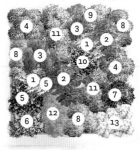

to grow: *Ophiopogon planiscapus* 'Nigrescens' (black mondo grass) forms rosettes of very dark evergreen blades.

- *Ruta graveolens* 'Jackman's Blue' (rue) is a small shrub with delicate, finely indented, silvery blue foliage.

LOCATION
Exposure: Gentle sun, light partial shade.
Position: This foliage wall will look very impressive on a terrace, large balcony, or patio, or in a small courtyard.

1. *Stachys byzantina* 'Silver Carpet'
2. *Hosta* 'Honeybells'
3. *Imperata cylindrica* 'Red Baron'
4. *Phalaris arundinacea* 'Feesey'
5. *Heuchera* 'Black Beauty'
6. *Ajuga reptans* 'Burgundy Glow'
7. *Ophiopogon planiscapus* 'Nigrescens'
8. *Ruta graveolens* 'Jackman's Blue'
9. *Helichrysum italicum*
10. *Ajuga reptans* 'Atropurpurea'
11. *Artemisia schmidtiana* 'Nana'
12. *Heuchera* 'Citronelle'
13. *Heuchera villosa*

PLANTING

When to plant: From March to May.

How to plant: Take out the root balls and remove as much soil as possible, keeping just the minimum around the roots. Place each plant in a pocket, pressing down well, and then staple the edges of the pockets, if necessary, so that the roots adhere firmly to the wall.

MAINTENANCE

Structure:

- Check daily to make sure there is no problem with the watering, such as weak or dead batteries in the programmer, incorrect programming, or water supply cut off.

   - Check the dosage of nutrients regularly.

Plants:

- Reed canary grass, *Phalaris arundinacea* 'Feesey', is dormant from December to March. Carefully remove the leaves when they die off.

   - Leave the dried stems of *Imperata cylindrica* 'Red Baron' in winter and remove them in spring when new shoots appear.

   - The leaves of hostas liquefy on the arrival of the first frosts: remove them immediately. In spring, when the first buds appear, put down some anti-slug pellets (Ferramol, compatible with organic gardening) on the ground, because slugs are particularly fond of hosta leaves.

   - The lamb's ear *Stachys byzantina* 'Silver Carpet', the lilyturf, the *Heuchera,* and the bugles require no care except to cut off any stems that are too long or going bare, and any damaged leaves.

   - During March, remove half the foliage of the *Artemisia,* the curry plant, and the rue (*Ruta graveolens*), to help keep these plants very compact. It will also lengthen their lives.

   - Regularly check the way all these plants spread out, to prevent the more invasive ones "eating" their neighbors. When they extend too far, just pull them out gently, being careful not to pull on the felt itself, and without damaging the parent plant and the plant next door.

LIFESPAN

The diverse colors of the leaves of these plants makes them as attractive as flowers, which does not prevent them from blooming—some discreetly and some in a striking manner.

The wall remains attractive in winter, because seven out of the ten plant species are evergreen. Moss will quickly take over any spaces left empty, giving unity to the whole.

Capable of living for decades if proper maintenance is carried out, this wall has it all. Don't forget that plants are living things and some may happen to die; in this case, you should replace them without qualms.

Below: *Hosta* 'Honeybells'

Opposite, top to bottom and left to right: *Helichrysum italicum* ssp. *serotinum, Ajuga reptans* 'Burgundy Glow', *Heuchera* 'Citronelle', *Stachys byzantina* 'Silver Carpet', *Artemisia schmidtiana* 'Nana', *Ruta graveolens* 'Jackman's Blue'.

MOSQUITO-REPELLENT WALL

Plants
- 6 southernwood, *Artemisia abrotanum*
- 10 *Thymus pseudolanuginosus*
- 6 lemon balm, *Melissa officinalis*
- 6 lemon verbena, *Aloysia citrodora*
- 6 lemon-scented geraniums, *Pelargonium crispum*
- 6 small leaf basil

PREPARATION TIME:
STRUCTURE: 1½ DAYS
PLANTING: 4 HOURS

Once the weather gets fine and there is a combination of heat and humidity, mosquitoes start to attack certain types of skin. Drive them away with citrus-scented plants: there is nothing they hate more!

VERTICAL GARDEN CONCEPT
Surface: A wall 3 feet (1 m) wide by 7 feet (2 m) high.
Planting: In pockets.
Maintenance: Watering, controlled by a programmer, delivering diluted fertilizer through perforated pipes from the top of the wall.

SELECTED PLANTS
The wormwood, with the common name of southernwood (*Artemisia abrotanum*), is a very fine, pearl-gray perennial evergreen.

Woolly thyme (*Thymus pseudolanuginosus*) spreads very quickly by creeping, and its purple flowers, which appear in June, almost entirely cover its tiny gray leaves.

Lemon balm (*Melissa officinalis*), is a perennial with light green foliage. There is a variety with golden leaves, and another with green and yellow variegated foliage.

LOCATION
Exposure: Sun.
Position: This wall could be installed on a balcony or terrace, near where you sit outside to rest, sunbathe, or have meals. It can be effective placed near to doors and windows, too.

PLANTING
When to plant: May.
How to plant: Take out the root balls and

1. Basil
2. *Artemisia abrotanum*
3. Lemon balm *Melissa officinalis*
4. Lemon verbena *Aloysia citrodora*
5. *Thymus pseudolanuginosus*
6. Lemon-scented geranium *Pelargonium crispum*

remove as much soil as possible. Place each plant in a pocket, pressing down well, and then staple the edges of the pockets so that the roots adhere firmly to the wall.

MAINTENANCE
Structure:
- Check daily to make sure there is no problem with the watering, such as weak or dead batteries in the programmer, incorrect programming, or water supply cut off.
- Check the dosage of nutrients regularly.

Plants:
- In March, reduce the clump of wormwood by half. Do the same to the thyme.
- Lemon balm dies back in winter, but comes back again in force in the spring. Reduce the volume in late June and again in September.

The lemon verbena and scented geranium are of only average hardiness. If they do not revive after the winter, change them.

Replant basil every year in May.

Do not allow any of these plants to flower, except the thyme and geranium, as this would be detrimental to their foliage.

If a plant spreads out too much, gently pull it out.

HARVEST
Pick basil, lemon verbena, and lemon balm from May to October. Thyme can be picked throughout the year.

LIFESPAN
This wall is especially attractive in summer, when all the plants are actively growing and when the mosquitoes are waiting to bite you!

In winter, half the plants are dormant. Lemon balm, thyme, and wormwood will live for many years. The same goes for lemon verbena and geranium if you live in an area where the winters are not too harsh.

EPICUREAN WALL

Plants (perennials)
- 7 perennial rocket
- 6 ever-bearing strawberries
- 6 June-bearing strawberries
- 5 sorrels with leaves of different colors
- 5 Good King Henry
- 10 navelwort</box>

PREPARATION TIME:
STRUCTURE: 1½ DAYS
PLANTING: 4 HOURS

With this wall, you will have salads, vegetables, and strawberries, all within easy reach! And even if your balcony is tiny, you will always have some goodies to harvest throughout the year.

VERTICAL GARDEN CONCEPT

Surface: A wall 3 feet (1 m) wide by 7 feet (2 m) high.

Planting: In pockets.

Maintenance: Watering, controlled by a programmer, delivering diluted fertilizer through perforated pipes from the top of the wall.

SELECTED PLANTS

- Perennial rocket is a herbaceous plant growing 8 to 12 inches (20–30 cm) tall, and to 24 or 27.5 inches (60–70 cm) when flowering.

- Strawberry plants look very decorative, with their dark green leaves, little white flowers, and red fruit.

- Sorrel, with its large leaves—broad and thick, colored bright green and blood red—grows in large clumps out of which extend green or purple flower panicles. Here are some species and varieties: *Rumex acetosa* is common sorrel (the broad-leaved 'Belleville' is the most widely grown in France; 'Verte de Nonay'; 'Blonde de Lyon'; 'De Chambourcy'; and 'Large de Belleville'), *Rumex montanus* var. *purpurea, Rumex scutatus.*

- Good King Henry is a wild plant, common in the European countryside. Nor-

mally it is from 12 to 20 inches (30–50 cm) tall, but it can grow to a height of 3 feet (1 m). The leaves are petiolate, alternate, smooth-edged, and triangular, dark green, with the undersides covered with a light, floury dust. You could collect a few wild specimens in the countryside, or buy them from a specialist seed merchant.

- Navelwort (*Umbilicus rupestris*), a small, chubby-looking plant, is often seen growing on old mossy roofs, embankments, and walls in some regions of France (the South, Brittany). If you come across navelwort when out walking, you can take a few specimens to plant; if, as is often the case, they are firmly stuck between two stones, use a pointed knife, being careful not to damage the roots.

LOCATION

Exposure: Gentle sun, light partial shade.

Position: This wall is ideal for a balcony.

PLANTING

When to plant: From March to May.

How to plant: Take out the root balls and remove as much soil as possible, keeping just the minimum around the roots. Place each plant in a pocket, pressing down well, and then staple the edges of the pockets, if necessary, so that the roots adhere firmly to the wall.

MAINTENANCE

Structure:

- Check daily to make sure there is no problem with the watering, such as weak or dead batteries in the programmer, incorrect programming, or water supply cut off.

- Check the dosage of nutrients regularly.

Plants:

- Cut off withered leaves regularly.

- Do not allow the sorrel, rocket, and Good King Henry to bolt.

- Keep an eye on the different clumps, to discipline them and to make sure they

1. Ever-bearing strawberries
2. Good King Henry
3. Navelwort
4. Perennial rocket
5. Sorrel
6. June-bearing strawberries

do not take over their neighbors' territory. When they extend too far, just pull them out gently, being careful not to pull on the felt itself, and without damaging the parent plant and the plant next door.

- In midsummer, if it is very hot and there is a drying wind, add an extra three-minute watering to the regular program during the afternoon between two programmed irrigations, or water the wall yourself using a fine mist spray.

If, in the growing season, a plant shows signs of weakness, cut it back to 1 inch (3 cm) from the base to help it take off again. If new shoots do not appear after fifteen days, gently remove the root ball from the pocket and replace the plant. But it is quite normal for some plants to be dormant in winter. The navelwort, on the other hand, rests during the summer, so be careful not to pull the plants up thinking they are dead.

- Runners from the strawberry plants quickly colonize the space. Do not let them invade neighboring plants.

HARVEST

- Wild rocket is hardy and perennial; it can be picked from March to November, and throughout the year in a mild climate or if the wall is well sheltered. Harvest it by cutting off leaves with scissors; do this regularly to keep the plants low-growing and thick.

- If you choose June-bearing strawberry varieties, they will reward you with a single, abundant crop in May and June. Ever-bearing varieties will give you smaller crops, but will continue bearing fruit until the first frosts.

- Sorrel can be harvested from March to November; pick the leaves as you need them.

A little cookery

- Rocket: The pungent flavor is refreshing and very special, recalling watercress and hazelnut. The young raw leaves are tender and can be mixed in with other salads, such as green salads, tomato salads, and pasta salads. They can accompany meat and poultry, and can completely transform an ordinary sandwich! Cooked, they can be used to enliven sauces and soups.

- Strawberries: Fresh, in jams, preserves, tarts, as juice . . . it's up to you to choose and be inventive.

- Sorrel: Delicious in omelets, as soup, as an accompaniment to fish, and to enhance the flavor of spinach or goosefoot. Finely chopped young raw leaves can be used to liven up a green salad.

- Good King Henry: This wild plant is a delicious vegetable that can be prepared and cooked in a similar way to spinach.

- Navelwort: This is a delicious winter salad to eat alone or mix with other green leaves such as lamb's lettuce and dandelions. The leaves are somewhat waxy, thick, and juicy.

- Harvest the leaves of Good King Henry from April to November.

- The little round leaves of the navelwort appear from September to May; the plants are dormant during the summer.

LIFESPAN

The plants selected are all perennials. They can therefore live for several years in this vertical garden, or even for decades if you look after them well and replace those that show signs of weakness.

In winter, some of the plants are dormant; on the other hand, the navelworts are at the peak of their growth.

There is nothing to stop you from using your own ideas and replacing some of these plants with others, but be careful to choose ones with superficial roots rather than taproots; it would be hard to imagine root crops, such as horseradishes and carrots, growing on a wall!

Navelwort growing between the stones of a wall.

Left, top to bottom: Sorrel, Good King Henry.

Right, top to bottom: Strawberry, rocket.

AROMATIC HERB WALL

Plants
- 2 shrub rosemary
- 3 trailing rosemary
- 6 trailing savory
- 2 lemon verbena
- 6 mint
- 6 lemon balm
- 2 hyssop
- 3 scarlet bee balm
- 1 *Agastache*
- 5 oregano
- 5 thyme
- 3 *Calamintha*

PREPARATION TIME:
STRUCTURE: 1½ DAYS
PLANTING: 4 HOURS

To have all the herbs you need at your fingertips is a dream for the gardener as well as for the cook. They are perfect for flavoring your cooking and for concocting delicious herbal teas.

VERTICAL GARDEN CONCEPT
Surface: A wall 3 feet (1 m) wide by 7 feet (2 m) high.
Planting: In pockets.
Maintenance: Watering, controlled by a programmer, delivering diluted fertilizer through perforated pipes from the top of the wall.

SELECTED PLANTS
All the plants chosen are perennials or shrubs and do not have taproots. If you replace some plants with others, avoid planting sage; it does not like growing on this type of wall and will very quickly die.
- The flowers of rosemary (*Rosmarinus officinalis*) are mostly blue-purple, but may be pink or white for less common varieties. Normally its habit is upright and bushy, but the trailing growth habit of *Rosmarinus* 'Prostratus' is very effective when the plant is grown vertically.
- Creeping savory is well suited to this type of wall. *Satureja alternipilosa*, a creeping savory with countless tiny white flowers appearing in midsummer, we have chosen here because of the elegant way it spreads over the support all by itself.
Lemon balm (*Melissa officinalis*), is perennial, with light green foliage. There is also a variety with golden leaves, and another with green and yellow variegated foliage.

Hyssop produces beautiful purple flower spikes. And you can enjoy its semi-evergreen foliage all year round.
- Hummingbird mint (*Agastache*), calamint (*Calamintha*), and bee balm (*Monarda*) are normally sold as ornamental plants, but their flavors and fragrances are just as interesting as those of classic aromatic plants, and, in addition, their visual aspect enlivens and adorns this wall in a flamboyant manner.
- Here are some species and varieties of oregano: *Origanum vulgare*, the most common species, with purple flowers ('Aureum crispum' a dwarf golden oregano; 'Kent Beauty', highly decorative with its pink bracts; 'Compactum', very good for covering the surface; and 'Polyphant', with variegated foliage and white flowers.)
- You can choose to plant different sorts of thyme: *Thymus vulgaris*, common thyme; *T. citriodorus*, thyme with a strong scent of lemon ('Aureus', lemon-scented with golden foliage; 'Bertram Anderson', lemon-scented, chartreuse green foliage); *T. serpyllum*, wild thyme, which spreads and creeps; and *T. pseudolanuginosus*, woolly thyme, which creeps and hangs down.

LOCATION
Exposure: Gentle sun.
Position: This wall can be installed in a garden, on a terrace, or on a balcony.

1. Mint
2. Lemon balm
3. *Agastache*
4. Scarlet bee balm
5. *Calamintha*
6. Shrub rosemary
7. Trailing rosemary
8. Thyme
9. Trailing savory
10. Oregano
11. Lemon verbena
12. Hyssop

Beware of the cold
If a freezing spell is forecast, staple a protective sheet of nonwoven fabric (frost protection fleece) to the top of the wall, and carefully fix it in place at the bottom, anchoring it with flowerpots, for instance.

A little cookery

- The flavor of rosemary is persistent, herbaceous, camphorated, pungent, and bitter: cook with both flowers and leaves, fresh or dried, whole or ground, with grilled meat, in *bouquet garni*, or as herb tea.

- The spicy and phenolated flavor of savory harmonizes perfectly with game, rabbit, salads, soups, and starchy foods.

- Lemon verbena has a very fine, lemony flavor. It is perfect as an infusion, hot or cold, and adds a pleasant flavor to dairy desserts, fruit salads, and liqueurs.

- Fresh, mentholated, slightly spicy, the classic flavor of mint is well known. But the scents and tastes of different mint varieties are endless. Use in salads, with peas, potatoes, zucchini (courgettes), and cucumbers, in omelets, in fruit salads; not to mention herbal teas and drinks of all kinds.

- The flavor of lemon balm is a subtle blend of lemon and mint. It harmonizes with fish, fruit salads, and dairy desserts.

- Used raw, finely chopped leaves of hyssop are delicious in salads. Cooked, it is perfect with game, pork, and soups. It also adds a delicate flavor to apricot or peach tarts.

- Use finely chopped scarlet bee balm in salads and pizzas; its flavor, reminiscent of bergamot, also works wonders with zucchini (courgettes), tomatoes, and eggplant (aubergines).

- *Agastache rugosa* has a mentholated flavor and *Agastache foeniculum* the scent of anise; use either or both of them in green salads, fruit salads, omelets . . . and herbal teas, of course.

- The fresh or dried leaves of oregano, and the flowers, have a spicy and slightly bitter taste. They are used to flavor pizzas, meat sauces, pasta, salads, and more.

- The archetypal *herbe de Provence*, thyme is delicious with grilled meats, in salads and marinades, with cheese, and, of course, it is an essential ingredient of the famous *bouquet garni*. Both leaves and flowers can be used in cooking.

The menthol flavor of *Calamintha* accompanies green salads, fruit salads, dairy desserts, and ice cream, and it is exquisite as an herbal tea.

PLANTING

When to plant: From March to May.

How to plant: Take out the root balls and remove as much soil as possible, keeping just the minimum around the roots. Place each plant in a pocket, pressing down well, and then staple the edges of the pockets, if necessary, so that the roots adhere firmly to the wall.

MAINTENANCE

Structure:

- Check daily to make sure there is no problem with the watering, such as weak or dead batteries in the programmer, incorrect programming, or water supply cut off.

- Check the dosage of nutrients regularly.

Plants:

- Cut off leaves of mint, lemon balm, oregano, bee balm, *Agastache,* and *Calamintha* as soon as they start to go yellow.

- Remove wilted flowers of *Agastache*, bee balm, *Calamintha,* and lemon verbena.

- Lemon verbena is not very hardy. If you do not live in a zone with a mild climate, cut it right back in late October and cover the stump with a pouch of frost protection fleece, pinned to the felt.

- Do not let the lemon balm flower: it will seed itself and spread where it is not wanted.

HARVEST

- Rosemary blooms very early in spring, or even in late winter. It can be picked all year round. The flowers, as well as the leaves, can be used.

- The leaves of trailing savory can be picked all year round. The white flowers appear in September, and have a delicate flavor.

- Pick lemon verbena leaves from April to October, and the flowers in August and September.

- Mint leaves can be picked from April right through to October, so long as the foliage is cut back in late June, just after flowering.

- Pick lemon balm from May to October; it is at its best, however, in June, and also in September so long as the plant has been cut back at the end of June.

- Hyssop produces its magnificent purple flower spikes from June to September. Its semi-evergreen foliage can be picked throughout the year.

- The leaves of the scarlet bee balm can be picked from May to October and its spectacular flowers during the summer.

- With *Agastache*, pick the leaves from May to October and the flowers in summer.

- Pick the leaves of your oregano as you need them, from May to October, and the flowers in summer.

- The small, intensely flavored leaves of thyme can be picked all year long. Pick the flowers from June to August.

- The leaves of *Calamintha* can be picked from May to October, and its flowers from July to September.

LIFESPAN
This vertical garden can live for many years so long as maintenance is carried out regularly, for both the structure and the plants.

Right, from top to bottom: Hyssop, lemon balm, bee balm *Monarda* 'Prairieglut'.

PERFUMED WALL

Plants
- 6 dame's rocket
- 10 basket of gold
- 15 pinks
- 6 August lily
- 10 evergreen candytuft
- 6 lavender
- 6 bee balm
- 6 *Santolina*
- 3 trailing rosemary
- 3 shrub rosemary
- 9 curry plant
- 6 *Agastache*

PREPARATION TIME:
STRUCTURE: 2 DAYS
PLANTING: 8 HOURS

VERTICAL GARDEN CONCEPT
Surface: A wall 7 feet (2 m) wide by 7 feet (2 m) high.
Planting: In pockets.
Maintenance: Watering, controlled by a programmer, delivering diluted fertilizer through perforated pipes from the top of the wall.

SELECTED PLANTS
- A short-lived perennial, dame's rocket (*Hesperis matronalis*), has a sweet and heady scent, particularly in the evening, and looks a little like a wallflower. Flowers are mauve or white, and the plant is 24 to 31 inches (60–80 cm) tall.
- A great classic of rockeries, the basket of gold (*Alyssum saxatile* or *Aurinia saxatile*) works wonderfully on a wall, where it will trail downward in a yellow, honey-scented carpet.
- With its long flowering period, peppery scent, and evergreen foliage, the pink (*Dianthus plumarius*) is full of merit. There are many varieties, from white to carmine, passing through all the different shades of pink. Choose two different ones, with three plants in each color.
- There are many different varieties of hostas, but the August lily, *Hosta plantaginea* 'Grandiflora', with white flowers, is the most fragrant. Moreover, it likes direct sunlight.
- With its copious honey-scented white flowers, evergreen candytuft (*Iberis sempervirens*) is spectacular in early spring.
- Choose two different varieties of lavender from among your favorites.
- Bee balms, whether *Monarda didyma* or *Monarda punctata*, have aromatic foliage. These perennials form tufts 31 inches (80 cm) high, and produce pleasantly dishevelled-looking flowers.
- *Santolina* with green or gray foliage? The choice is up to you. Both sorts are evergreen and scented, and produce yellow pompom flowers.

Aficionados of perfumes of all kinds will fall for this vertical garden, which mixes, at nose height, different fragrances over the seasons.

- Whether trailing or upright, rosemary blooms at the end of winter and sometimes can continue flowering until the first frosts.

- *Helichrysum italicum* ssp. *serotinum* is sometimes called the curry plant because of the incredible spicy fragrance given off by the foliage, just as much in sunshine as in rain.

- There are several different species and varieties of *Agastache*. Some have the scent—and taste—of menthol, and others of anise. Flowers are mauve, purple, raspberry pink, and apricot-colored. Choose two different sorts to plant.

1. *Hosta plantaginea* 'Grandiflora'
2. Dame's rocket
3. Trailing rosemary
4. Shrub rosemary
5. Lavender
6. Basket of gold
7. Evergreen candytuft
8. Bee balm
9. *Santolina*
10. *Agastache*
11. Curry plant
12. Pinks

LOCATION

Exposure: Sun.

Position: A place can be found for this wall almost anywhere: on a balcony or terrace, on a patio, or in a special corner of the garden, where you often sit (to rest or to have meals, for instance).

PLANTING

When to plant: From March to May.

How to plant: Take out the root balls and remove as much soil as possible, keeping just the minimum around the roots. Place each plant in a pocket, pressing down well, and then staple the edges of the pockets, if necessary, so that the roots adhere firmly to the wall.

MAINTENANCE

Structure:

- Check daily to make sure there is no problem with the watering, such as weak or dead batteries in the programmer, incorrect programming, or water supply cut off.

- Check the dosage of nutrients regularly.

Plants:

- Cut off wilted leaves and flowers regularly.

- Watch the different clumps, to limit them and to keep them from overlapping with neighboring plants. When they extend too far, just pull them out gently, without pulling on the felt itself.

- In high summer, if it is very hot and there is a drying wind, add an extra three-minute watering to the regular program during the afternoon between two programmed irrigations, or water the wall yourself using a fine mist spray.

- Cut off the flower spikes of dame's rocket as soon as they start to fade, to avoid tiring out the plant.

- In late May, cut off the wilted flowers of basket of gold and evergreen candytuft, and cut back half of the foliage, to keep the tufts from going thin at the base.

- When the flowers of the pinks wilt, cut them off and cut back half of the foliage.

- Cut of the wilted flowering stems of *Hosta plantaginea* 'Grandiflora', and remove the foliage as soon as it starts to liquefy in late autumn. Slugs are particularly fond of hostas, and are quite capable of climbing up a wall to get at them. Regularly put down on the ground some pellets of Ferramol, a natural anti-slug remedy that is not toxic to animals or birds.

- Each year in March, cut back half of the lavender's foliage, to stop it going thin at the base. Always prune above where new growth is appearing, and never on dead wood.

- When bee balm has finished blooming, cut back its foliage to 4 inches (10 cm); new leaves will then appear very quickly.

- Cut back the stems of *Santolina* by half in March.

- Rosemary plants grow in an attractive

way all by themselves; there is no need to touch them.

- Every spring, in March, prune back all the stems of the curry plant by half, making sure always to cut above where new growth is appearing.

- Cut back the foliage of *Agastache* after flowering, to give it a chance to recuperate.

FLOWERING

Flowering is spread out over the year:

- At the very beginning of spring, the rosemary, followed by the basket of gold and the evergreen candytuft.

- Then from May to July, the pinks.

- In summer and autumn, the dame's rocket, *Agastache*, *Santolina,* and hosta.

- In winter, almost all the foliage is evergreen, except for the dame's rocket, hosta, bee balm, and *Agastache*.

LIFESPAN

All these perennial plants live for many years, except for the short-lived dame's rocket, which only lives for a maximum of three to four years.

Opposite: Basket of gold, *Agastache* 'Blue Fortune'

Top left: *Hosta plantaginea* 'Grandiflora'

Right, from top to bottom: Pink *Dianthus* 'Lily the Pink', *Santolina rosmarinifolia*

A WALL OF MOSSES . . .
OR ALMOST!

Plants (perennials)
- 5 *Soleirolia soleirolii*
- 5 *Acaena buchananii*
- 6 mountain sandwort, *Are-naria montana*
- 5 *Leptinella dioica*
- 5 moss phlox, *Phlox subulata* 'Bonita'
- 8 County Park Pratia (*Pratia pedunculata* 'County Park')
- 6 heath pearlwort (*Sagina subulata*)
- 7 goldmoss stonecrop (*Sedum acre* 'Elegans')
- 5 saxifrage (*Saxifraga apicu-lata* 'Gregor Mendel')

PREPARATION TIME:
STRUCTURE: 1½ DAYS
PLANTING: 4 HOURS

This looks like a vertical garden just made of moss! With their tiny leaves, the plants chosen form a carpet and blend with the mosses, which grow naturally on the felt.

VERTICAL GARDEN CONCEPT
Surface: For a wall 3 feet (1 m) wide by 7 feet (2 m) high.
Planting: In pockets.
Maintenance: Watering, controlled by a programmer, delivering diluted fertilizer through perforated pipes from the top of the wall.

SELECTED PLANTS
All these plants have evergreen leaves, so the vertical garden, placed near a window—on a balcony, for instance—will be decorative all year round. From March to July there are flowers to enliven the general effect, each plant blooming in turn. There are even amusing little fruits, those of the *Acaena*, which appear in autumn.

- *Soleirolia soleirolii* (Baby's tears, formerly called *Helxine soleirolii*) looks adorable with its tiny round bright green leaves, growing over the felt like a mossy carpet. It grows no taller than 1 inch (3 cm).
- With its light gray-green foliage, *Acaena buchananii* forms a dense carpet 3 inches (8 cm) high.
- Sandwort (*Arenaria montana*) grows in big dark green cushions, 4 inches (10 cm) high.

The plant now called *Leptinella dioica*

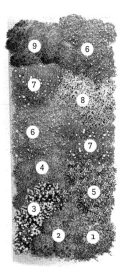

1. *Soleirolia soleirolii*
2. *Acaena buchananii*
3. *Arenaria montana*
4. *Leptinella dioica*
5. *Phlox subulata* 'Bonita'
6. *Pratia pedunculata* 'County Park'
7. *Sagina subulata*
8. *Sedum acre* 'Elegans'
9. *Saxifraga apiculata* 'Gregor Mendel'

was until recently considered part of the *Cotula* genus. With its pretty leaves, small and very jagged, it forms a low carpet 2 inches (5 cm) high.

- *Phlox subulata* 'Bonita' is 4 inches (10 cm) high, and forms a compact mass of vegetation.
- Very carpet-like, *Pratia pedunculata* 'County Park' never grows higher than 1 inch (3 cm).
- Sometimes pearlwort (*Sagina subulata*; see photo below) is sold in blocks! It really does look like moss, growing 2 inches (5 cm) high.
- The plump little light green leaves of *Sedum acre* 'Elegans' will grow no taller than 4 inches (10 cm) in height.
- *Saxifraga apiculata* 'Gregor Mendel' (saxifrage) grows in a firm, dense cushion, with gray-green foliage, 4 inches (10 cm) high.

LOCATION
Exposure: Gentle sunlight.
Position: This vertical garden will do best in a small space, well sheltered from wind and severe frosts; on a patio, terrace, or balcony. It forms a "plant picture" that never grows more than 4 inches (10 cm) thick. But don't forget that it still needs sunlight!

PLANTING

When to plant: From March to May.

How to plant: Take out the root balls and remove as much soil as possible, keeping just the minimum around the roots.

Place each plant in a pocket, pressing down well, and then staple the edges of the pockets, if necessary, so that the roots adhere firmly to the wall.

MAINTENANCE

Structure:

- Check daily to make sure there is no problem with the watering, such as weak or dead batteries in the programmer, incorrect programming, or water supply cut off.

- Check the dosage of nutrients regularly.

Plants:

- Be careful, as all these plants spread rapidly. Check the tufts to limit them and to prevent them from taking over their neighbors. Even if one or other of them delights you with how rapidly it grows, don't let it invade others beyond its territory. When one of the plants extends too far, just pull it up gently, without pulling on the felt itself, and making sure not to damage the parent plant and neighboring plants.

- In midsummer, if it is very hot and there is a drying wind, add an extra three-minute watering to the regular program during the afternoon between two programmed irrigations, or water the wall yourself using a fine mist spray.

- Cut off wilted flowers and damaged leaves with scissors.

- All these plants have evergreen foliage. After a hard winter, some, such as *Soleirolia soleirolii*, may lose their leaves. If all is well, they should take off again in April, but if they have still shown no signs of life by the time May comes along, replace them.

FLOWERING

- The flowers of *Acaena buchananii* look insignificant, but they turn into amusing little lime-green fruits in autumn.

- Mountain sandwort (*Arenaria montana*) produces surprisingly large and copious white flowers from May to July.

- The small yellow ochre flowers of *Leptinella dioica* appear in May and June.

- *Phlox subulata* 'Bonita' flowers with small mauve corollas in April and May.

- When the copious deep blue star-shaped flowers of *Pratia pedunculata* 'County Park' appear, from May to July, it is difficult to see anything else!

- Pearlwort (*Sagina subulata*) is covered in miniature white flowers in June and July.

- Goldmoss stonecrop (*Sedum acre* 'Elegans') is a variety of wallpepper and produces flowers, in a lighter color than the species plant's lemon yellow, from May to July.

- *Saxifraga apiculata* 'Gregor Mendel' is covered in delightful pale yellow flowers in March and April.

LIFESPAN

If you live in a zone with a mild climate, all these plants will live for many years.

Soleirolia soleirolii can be killed by the cold, but this is not a reason to deny yourself the pleasure of growing it, for it is a really interesting plant when grown on this type of support. Simply replace it, if necessary, each spring. It is cheap to buy and grows so quickly that within two months it will once again be occupying its original space.

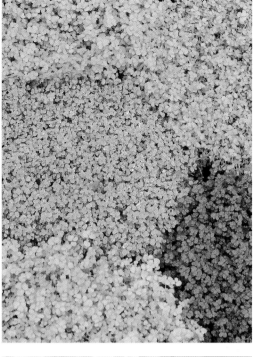

Opposite: *Pratia pedunculata*

Left, from top to bottom: *Soleirolia soleirolii, Sedum acre* 'Elegans'.

Right, from top to bottom: *Arenaria montana, Saxifraga apiculata* 'Gregor Mendel', *Sagina subulata* 'Aurea'.

A WALL OF FERNS

Plants
(potted specimens only)
- 13 *Phyllitis scolopendrium*
- 10 *Phyllitis scolopendrium* 'Cristata'
- 6 *Polystichum setiferum*
- 4 *Polystichum setiferum* 'Plumosum Densum'
- 7 *Dryopteris erythrosora*

PREPARATION TIME:
STRUCTURE: 2 DAYS
PLANTING: 8 HOURS

VERTICAL GARDEN CONCEPT
Surface: For a wall 7 feet (2 m) wide by 7 feet (2 m) high.
Planting: In pockets.
Maintenance: Watering, controlled by a programmer, delivering diluted fertilizer through perforated pipes from the top of the wall.

SELECTED PLANTS
These ferns have evergreen leaves with varied colors and shapes, alternating particularly fine or even feathery fronds with others like shiny ribbons. Furthermore, these plants grow rapidly, forming handsome clumps that always look healthy.

- *Phyllitis scolopendrium* (hart's tongue fern), has long, narrow, smooth-edged fronds that look like bright shiny light green ribbons. It grows to about 16 to 20 inches (40–50 cm) in all directions.

- The hart's tongue fern variety *Phyllitis scolopendrium* 'Cristata' does not grow bigger than 12 inches (30 cm). The long, smooth-edged fronds have crests along their edges and are indented at the ends. The effect is of curly and shiny light green lettuce leaves.

- The dark green, finely serrated fronds of *Polystichum setiferum* (soft shield fern) are up to 20 inches (50 cm) long and spread out to form handsome clumps.

- The variety *Polystichum setiferum* 'Plumosum Densum' (soft shield fern) is the same height, but the light green fronds are dense and feathery.

- The triangular fronds of *Dryopteris erythrosora* (autumn fern) are coppery, sometimes almost baby pink, in spring when they first appear, and then they turn a shiny dark green. The foliage disappears completely in early spring, but new fronds appear immediately. Height 24 inches (60 cm).

If you would like to opt for other kinds of fern, choose species with evergreen fronds, and go for contrast: fine, feathery, broad, dark green, luminous green, etc.

Ferns have incomparable strength and subtlety. And when they are evergreen, like the ones in this vertical garden, they brave the winter in style!

LOCATION

Exposure: Gentle sunlight or light shade. A western exposure is ideal.

Position: If you have a location that is well lit, without being exposed completely to the south, why not choose this spectacular vertical garden, which remains green all year? Install it on a patio or terrace, or in a courtyard or a garden.

PLANTING

When to plant: In spring or autumn.
How to plant: It is vital to take particular

1. *Phyllitis scolopendrium* 'Cristata'
2. *Polystichum setiferum*
3. *Phyllitis scolopendrium*
4. *Dryopteris erythrosora*
5. *Polystichum setiferum* 'Plumosum Densum'

care with the design. Draw soft diagonal lines and curves with chalk, and then make your incisions, taking care that the plants are always in staggered rows from one line to the next. Take out the root balls and remove as much soil as possible, keeping just the minimum around the roots. Place each plant in a pocket, pressing down well, and then staple the edges of the pockets, if necessary, so that the roots adhere firmly to the wall.

MAINTENANCE
Structure:
- Check daily to make sure there is no problem with the watering, such as weak or dead batteries in the programmer, incorrect programming, or water supply cut off.
  - Check the dosage of nutrients regularly.

Plants:
- In midsummer, when it is very hot, water all the foliage using a fine mist spray; always water in the evening. Add an extra watering to the regular program if necessary, in mid-afternoon. You can quickly see for yourself if the felt is drying out: it becomes like cardboard.
  - The fronds of evergreen ferns often dry out in springtime and are replaced with new ones. You can cut them off with scissors as they die back, to keep the wall looking neat and tidy. In fact you can do this all year long, as soon as a leaf turns yellow.

LIFESPAN
This is a vertical garden you will enjoy for several years, or even several decades if you maintain it regularly. Thanks to the evergreen foliage of the ferns, it looks decorative and lively right through the year.

Left, from top to bottom: *Phyllitis scolopendrium* 'Cristata', *Phyllitis scolopendrium* 'Crispum'.

Opposite:
Top left: *Phyllitis scolopendrium*.
Top right: *Dryopteris erythrosora*.
Bottom: *Polystichum setiferum*.

BLACK-AND-WHITE CHECKERBOARD

Plants
- 20 black mondo grass, *Ophiopogon planiscapus* 'Nigrescens'
- 20 coral bells, *Heuchera* 'Blackout'
- 20 silver mound, *Artemisia schmidtiana* 'Nana'
- 20 lamb's ear, *Stachys byzantina* 'Silver Carpet'

VERTICAL GARDEN CONCEPT
Surface: For a wall 7 feet (2 m) wide by 7 feet (2 m) high.
Planting: In pockets.
Maintenance: Watering, controlled by a programmer, delivering diluted fertilizer through perforated pipes from the top of the wall.

SELECTED PLANTS
We have chosen these plants because of their evergreen or semi-evergreen foliage and their strong tones, and because they are easy to grow. But there is nothing to stop you looking through nursery catalogs to find other alternatives, always bearing in mind that they should be either very dark or very light, and should grow in fairly low clumps.

Stachys byzantina 'Silver Carpet'.

- *Ophiopogon planiscapus* 'Nigrescens' (or 'Niger'), black mondo grass, grows 8 inches (20 cm) high and forms dense carpets. The foliage, in the form of blades, is perhaps the darkest of those currently available as garden plants, and is evergreen.

- 'Blackout' is the blackest of all the coral bells. Its flowers are white and pinkish, and stand out dramatically against the dark foliage with its shiny, wavy, almost round leaves. Its habit always remains very compact, and the plant measures 16 inches (40 cm) in all directions.

- *Artemisia schmidtiana* 'Nana' is a dwarf variety of silver mound with semi-evergreen, very finely serrated silver leaves and creeping stems. It is 4 inches (10 cm) high and will spread out over 12 inches (30 cm).

- *Stachys byzantina* 'Silver Carpet' forms a particularly spectacular-looking

In a contemporary garden or on the terrace of an apartment, a checkerboard made of squares of plants with almost black foliage, alternated with others that have silver, practically white leaves, can look very original.

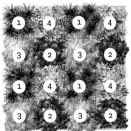

1. *Ophiopogon planiscapus* 'Nigrescens'
2. *Heuchera* 'Blackout'
3. *Artemisia schmidtiana* 'Nana'
4. *Stachys byzantina* 'Silver Carpet'

woolly carpet of silver leaves. It is evergreen or semi-evergreen and does not flower, which means it always has a neat and tidy appearance. Its common name is lamb's ear. It grows 6 inches (15 cm) tall, but it will spread out over 24 inches (60 cm) if you let it!

LOCATION
Exposure: Sunny.
Position: This vertical garden has a very contemporary look, and would go very well with the clean lines and smooth walls of

modern "architect-designed" houses. We advise you to resist its temptations if you live in a traditional, old-fashioned house, or one with stone walls.

PLANTING

When to plant: In spring, but autumn is possible too.

How to plant: Draw vertical and horizontal lines 20 inches (50 cm) apart. This will give you sixteen 20-inch (50 cm) squares. Make five pockets per square: four in each corner and one in the middle. Number the squares from top to bottom and from left to right. Take out the root balls and remove as much soil as possible, keeping just the minimum around the roots. Plant *Ophiopogon* in squares 1, 3, 9, and 11. Plant *Stachys* in squares 2, 4, 10, and 12. Plant *Artemisia* in squares 5, 7, 13, and 15. Plant *Heuchera* in squares 6, 8, 14, and 16. Place a plant in each pocket, pressing down well, and then staple the edges of the pockets, if necessary, so that the roots adhere firmly to the wall.

MAINTENANCE

Structure:

- Check daily to make sure there is no problem with the watering, such as weak or dead batteries in the programmer, incorrect programming, or water supply cut off.

　- Check the dosage of nutrients regularly.

Plants:

These plants hardly require any maintenance:

　- Remove damaged leaves and wilted flowers.

　- If a plant dies, replace it as soon as possible, to avoid "disturbing" the order of the composition.

　- Each year, in March, cut the *Artemisia* back slightly, to keep them nice and bushy.

　- During the same period, cut back the stems of the *Stachys* by half, if they are growing too much.

　- In general, keep a close eye on *Stachys* and *Artemisia*; both plants tend to try to invade their neighbors' territory.

FLOWERING

- *Ophiopogon* produces fine, pinkish white flowers from June to August, followed by little black berries.

　- *Heuchera* blooms with a fine mist of pinkish white flowers in June and July.

　- In summer, *Artemisia schmidtiana* 'Nana' can sometimes produce short clusters of small round pale yellow flower heads. Cut them off when they appear, to preserve the silver aspect of the plant, which is what gives it its charm

LIFESPAN

This vertical garden is made of plants that are easy to grow and to live with. It is capable of living for several years, or even decades.

Above, from top to bottom:
Artemisia schmidtiana 'Nana',
Heuchera 'Blackout'.

Opposite: *Ophiopogon*
planiscapus 'Nigrescens'.

"HOME-MADE" INSTALLATIONS

And now, with a bit of DIY and a dash of deco, here are some ways to show off your favorite plants!

COMPARTMENTS OF FERNS

**Plants
(in pots or containers)**
Outdoor ferns (hardy ones),
in different sizes

Materials
- A jigsaw or, even better, a
  circular saw
- A drill
- A level
- Sheets of marine plywood
  or recycled shelves
- Terracotta pots of different
  sizes
- Saucers to go under the
  pots
- Clay pellets
- Leaf mold

Imagine a bookcase where the books have been replaced with potted ferns! To decorate a north- or west-facing wall, build this wall of shelves and decorate it with plants.

Basic scenery design
Play around with the different volumes and sizes of plants. It is important to showcase each individual fern as though it were framed, and each one should have enough space to grow without too much restriction.

TECHNIQUE

Draw up a clear plan before you begin. The size of the structure depends on what you want and where it is located, but if it takes up an entire wall, it will look wonderful!

Build a kind of backless bookcase, with compartments of different sizes, just as you would do for books. Make sure to make it strong enough, because the pots and wet soil can be quite heavy. The wood must be thoroughly treated and sealed so it resists weather and spills from watering. It could be painted to match your garden furniture or the dominant tone of garden flowers. Drill several holes to fasten your "bookcase" securely to the wall

Some of the compartments can measure up to 28 inches (70 cm) square, others only 8 inches (20 cm); it is the mixture of different sizes that will give the composition its charm.

If you are not particularly good with your hands, explore flea markets and yard sales; you'll find indoor furniture designed to hold television sets, books, and other objects, or old bookcases with different sized compartments. Make sure the piece you have set your heart on is strong enough for the purpose. All that remains for you to do then is to treat, seal, and paint it.

SELECTED PLANTS

Ferns are woodland plants and do well grown in pots; obviously, they do not flower, but they have splendid foliage, ever-green for some species and varieties. There is a huge choice—here is a small selection:

- *Athyrium niponicum* 'Metallicum' (Japanese painted fern): The variegated fronds have blue and gray reflections, veined with purple, and are carried on petioles of the same color purple. Height 16 inches (40 cm).

- *Cyrtomium falcatum* (Japanese holly fern): The dark green shiny fronds are evergreen and form leathery, sickle-shaped divisions. Height 20 inches (50 cm).

- *Dryopteris erythrosora* (autumn fern): The young fronds are coppery, almost pink, and then they turn a shiny dark green over the months. Height 24 inches (60 cm).

- *Dryopteris* 'Cristata' (crested wood fern): The upright, light green fronds are short and wavy, measuring 24 inches (60 cm).

- *Onoclea sensibilis* (sensitive fern): This rhizomatous fern likes to grow in a wide dish. The broadly divided triangular light green fronds grow to 20 inches (50 cm).

- *Phyllitis scolopendrium* (hart's tongue fern): This fern grows 16 inches (40 cm) tall, with long, narrow, smooth-edged, and shiny light green fronds that are evergreen.

- *Phyllitis scolopendrium* 'Cristata' (hart's tongue fern): This variety is amusing, with fronds that have crests along their edges and are indented at the ends. It does not grow taller than 10 inches (25 cm).

- *Polypodium vulgare* (common polypody): This little fern does not grow taller than 8 inches (20 cm). It is evergreen and rhizomatous and has dark green, very glossy fronds with deep lobes.

- *Polystichum setiferum* (soft shield fern): With its evergreen, dark green, finely serrated fronds spreading out in all directions, this is a really interesting fern, particularly in winter. Height: 24 inches (60 cm). There are many hybrids, all of them magnificent.

LOCATION

Exposure: On a north- or west-facing wall, with sufficient light.

Position: This fern "bookcase" would look splendid on a balcony or terrace or in a city courtyard, but could also enliven an obscure, half-forgotten corner of the garden.

PLANTING
When to plant: All year round, but avoid periods of extreme heat or frost.
How to plant: Choose terracotta pots with a diameter slightly larger than the root balls. Put a layer of clay pellets in the bottom of each pot, then leaf mold. Finally, pot each fern in these containers.

MAINTENANCE
Structure:
Check regularly that the shelves are in good condition.

Plants:
- It is essential to keep ferns well watered, preferably, with rainwater; do not let the soil dry out between two waterings. Put saucers under the pots, but do not let water stagnate in them, unless you are going to be away for a few days, in which case you can fill up the saucers.
  - Cut off dried or damaged leaves regularly with scissors.
  - Repot your ferns each spring with leaf mold mixed with compost.
  - Top-dress only the plants that are in large pots.

LIFESPAN
If the wood has been thoroughly treated, this structure should last for many years. As for the ferns themselves, if they are well looked after and repotted regularly, they can live for a very long time.

Opposite: *Athyrium niponicum* 'Metallicum'

Above left: *Phyllitis scolopendrium* 'Cristata'.
Right, from top to bottom:
Dryopteris erythrosora,
Polystichum setiferum 'Cristatum'.

PATCHWORK
OF SUCCULENTS

Plants:
Different succulent plants:
Sedums, sempervivums,
saxifrages . . .

Materials:
- Terracotta flower pots
- System for attaching the
pots to the wall
- Potting soil and sand, or
special potting soil for succulents

PREPARATION TIME
4 HOURS

Cute, crisp, funny . . . there are endless adjectives to describe succulents. They are also easy to cultivate, so gardeners everywhere are tempted to grow them.

TECHNIQUE

Install terracotta pots very close together on a wall, attaching them either staggered or in straight rows. Before you start, consider the weight: the clay pot and the soil, combined with the irrigation water, can be very heavy. Do not neglect this aspect; choose suitable fastening systems.

Create the basic structure. It must be firmly fixed to the wall to support the weight of the pots and their contents. Several types of materials are suitable: Buy or scavenge rigid wire mesh, metal or wooden trellis, or interwoven metal strips. The important thing is to have a support that is firmly harnessed to the wall, so that neither the wind nor the weight of the pots can move it.

Once this structure is solidly anchored, you can leave it as it is or dress it up with wicker fencing or canvas made from plant fibers (flax, jute, hemp, etc.).

Finally, all that remains for you to do is to devise a system of hooks for the terracotta pots. For example, you can thread a thick wire through the hole at the bottom of the pot and shape it into a hook at the top to secure it to the support. Be careful not to block up the hole completely, as water must still be able to flow through it.

SELECTED PLANTS

These plants are attractive all through the year, even if some of them do not flower. Start with three or five plants, and then gradually add to your collection, choosing from *Sempervivum* (houseleeks or hen and chicks), stonecrop, and miniature saxifrages.

- *Sempervivums* are small succulent plants belonging to the Crassulaceae family. There are about forty species, and hundreds of hybrids. Their rosettes of closely packed, thick, pointed leaves vary in color from dark green and gray-green to almost blue, purple, and rust. They come in a multitude of different shapes. Gene-

rally they grow to between 2 and 6 inches (5–15 cm) tall. Flowers can be yellow, pink, or purple. Here are some varieties: *Sempervivum arachnoidium*, *Sempervivum calcareum*, *Sempervivum* 'Jubilee'.

- Still in the Crassulaceae family, stonecrops are perennials, often with a low, covering habit (which are the ones that interest us in this composition) although others are upright (such as *Sedum spectabile*, frequently seen in gardens). Low-growing stonecrops are from 2 to 6 inches (5–15 cm) tall, and flower with upright yellow, mauve, pink, or purple inflorescences. The fleshy foliage, very fine or almost round, can be gray-green, dark green, purple, rust, and even variegated.

Sedum acre 'Yellow Queen'

A judicious choice

As succulent plants remain compact and flatten themselves against their support, they are easy to grow in small pots. In addition, they do not require much watering, which makes their upkeep easier. Even when they are neglected they can survive, for their thick, fat leaves are able to retain the slightest drop of water.

Here are some varieties: *Sedum acre, Sedum aizoon, Sedum kamtschaticum, Sedum* 'Purpureum'.

- Saxifrages, which have given their name to the family of Saxifragaceae, need a little more water than the plants previously mentioned; otherwise they thin out from the center. They grow 2 to 6 inches (5–15 cm) tall, and form charming cushions of leaves, which can be fine and incised or fleshy. Many of them bloom with little white flowers, sometimes spotted with purple. Here are a few varieties: *Saxifraga hypnoides* 'Densa', *Saxifraga x arendsii, Saxifraga apiculata* 'Gregor Mendel', *Saxifraga juniperifolia.*

LOCATION

Exposure: Sun.

Position: This composition is perfect on a balcony or terrace, or in a courtyard or a garden, for instance on the gardener's shed. Be careful not to put the pots underneath a gutter; the water from it would quickly make the plants go rotten.

PLANTING

When to plant: From March to May.

How to plant: Put a layer of clay pellets or gravel in the bottom of each terracotta pot, and then add a light potting soil made of equal quantities of loam and sand. Place each plant in its pot, taking care not to bury the neck, for this would make it rot.

From top to bottom: *Saxifraga apiculata* 'Gregor Mendel', *Saxifraga hypnoides, Sedum aizoon.*

MAINTENANCE

- Wait for the soil to dry out before watering, if it does not rain.

  - Repot the plants every three years in a mixture of equal quantities of loam and sand, in well-drained pots with gravel in the bottom.

LIFESPAN

These plants are incredibly durable and can live for decades. To propagate them, don't hesitate to take cuttings, planting them very shallowly in pots filled with a mixture of equal quantities of loam and sand.

From top to bottom: *Sedum kamtschaticum* var. *floriferum* 'Weihenstephaner Gold', *Sempervivum arachnoïdium* 'Rubin', *Sempervivum calcareum* 'Limelight'.

CIRCLE OF *SEMPERVIVUMS*

Plants
3 different houseleeks in
4-inch (10 cm) pots

Materials:
- A round container 2 to 3
  inches (5–7 cm) deep, and
  about 12 inches (30 cm) in
  diameter, in a lightweight
  material such as zinc, aluminum, or stainless steel
- A drill with a fine bit, or a
  gimlet, depending on the
  material of the container
- Chicken wire
- Clay pellets
- Soil
- Wood moss
- Galvanized wire

PREPARATION TIME:
STRUCTURE: 1 HOUR
PLANTING: 30 MINUTES

TECHNIQUE

This little floral composition is very simple to make: a round container, serving as
a frame, is filled with clay pellets and soil
held in place by a fine mesh.

Drill eight holes ½ inch (1 cm) from the
edge: two at the top, 1 inch (2 cm) apart,
and the other six at 2 o'clock, 3 o'clock, 5
o'clock, 7 o'clock, 9 o'clock, and 10 o'clock.
Insert a wire through the top two holes;
this will be used to hang the composition
on the wall.

Place the chicken wire over the top of
the container. Wearing protective gloves,
and using a wire cutter, cut it out, leaving
a margin of about 1 inch (2 cm) around the
outside; this margin should be untwisted.
Solidify the whole assembly by twisting it
together again, using six lengths of galvanized wire, to go through the six holes you
drilled earlier. Fold the lengths of wire to
create a "table" with the same dimensions
as the container, into which it will fit.

With the container placed flat, poke
each "table leg" into its hole, but still leaving access to the inside of the container.
Fill the container with growing medium:
clay pellets and soil, with wood moss on
top, to within ½ inch (1 cm) of the top.

Lift up the container, gently pressing
the mesh until it is resting on the moss.
Mind your hands when the wires come out
through the back. If necessary, rework
the edges a bit so that the mesh perfectly
covers the soil. Finally, delicately pull the
wires from behind; the growing medium
must be well maintained but not crushed.
Twist the wires together to seal the cage:
9 o'clock with 3 o'clock, 10 o'clock with 5
o'clock, and 2 o'clock with 7 o'clock.

SELECTED PLANTS

With their evergreen foliage, houseleeks
are attractive all year round. Foliage can
be gray, silvery, purple, wine-colored,
bright green, or almost black. Depending
on species, the flowers can be red, pink,

We love these plants with their fleshy texture and incredible diversity. Grouped together in a picture like this, they transport us off into a variety of different lands.

yellow, or white, and they appear between May and October. The houseleeks sold in garden centers are decorative right away and are eminently suitable for this kind of stylistic exercise. They are easy to grow and can get by with very little soil and very little water. Just like camels, in fact!

LOCATION
Exposure: Sun.
Position: This little "plant picture" can be hung anywhere, alone or with others, so

In the same spirit, you could make a square or rectangular window, for example by recycling old canteen trays.

long as there is sun. So you could place it on a balcony, terrace, or patio. In the garden, you could hang it the door of a shed or barn; and, of course, on the front door, to welcome visitors.

Above: Sempervivum balcanicum

Opposite, top to bottom:
Sempervivum 'Reinhart',
Sempervivum ciliosum var. *Borisii.*

PLANTING

When to plant: All year.

How to plant: Place the container horizontally. Soak the potted plants for one minute in a basin of water. Remove some of the earth from around the roots, and then place the plants so you can judge the effect. To plant, cut the wire mesh in the chosen places with a small pair of wire cutters; remove the excess moss, push the earth aside to leave enough room for the roots, and install the plants. Fill in again, using a fork and small spoon for all these operations. Tamp down as much as possible, moisten the earth with a mist spray, and then put the moss back on top of the earth to help wedge the whole thing in place. Put back the cut edges of the wire mesh as close as possible to each plant.

MAINTENANCE

Every week, or twice a week if the weather is very hot, take down the container, place it flat on a table, and, using a spray, mist the growing medium with water at ambient temperature. Wait a few minutes before hanging it up again.

LIFESPAN

This decoration can only be temporary; it will last around three months. The soil, in this position, will begin to settle and mass together after a period of some weeks, and the plants will no longer be feeling completely comfortable after a few months. When the plants start to become unstable, do not hesitate to dig them up and replant them in the garden or a more conventional container. Put your frame away until next season, or use it again right away to create a whole new composition. You can rejuvenate your frame by painting it.

CIRCLE OF THYME

Plants
- 1 thyme *pseudolanuginosus*
- 1 thyme *serpyllum*
- 1 thyme *serpyllum* 'Albus'

Materials:
- A round container 2 to 3 inches (5–7 cm) deep, and about 12 inches (30 cm) in diameter, in a lightweight material such as zinc, aluminum, or stainless steel
- A drill with a fine bit, or a gimlet, depending on the material of the container
- Chicken wire
- Clay pellets
- Soil
- Wood moss
- Galvanized wire

PREPARATION TIME:
STRUCTURE: 1 HOUR
PLANTING: 30 MINUTES

TECHNIQUE

This little floral composition is very simple to make: a round container, serving as a frame, is filled with clay pellets and soil held in place by a fine mesh.

Drill eight holes ½ inch (1 cm) from the edge: two at the top, 1 inch (2 cm) apart, and the other six at 2 o'clock, 3 o'clock, 5 o'clock, 7 o'clock, 9 o'clock, and 10 o'clock. Insert a wire through the top two holes: this will be used to hang the composition on the wall.

Place the chicken wire over the top of the container. Wearing protective gloves, and using a wire cutter, cut it out, leaving a margin of about 1 inch (2 cm) around the outside; this margin should be untwisted. Solidify the whole assembly by twisting it together again, using six lengths of galvanized wire, to go through the six holes you drilled earlier. Fold the lengths of wire to create a "table" with the same dimensions as the container, into which it will fit.

With the container placed flat, poke each "table leg" into its hole, but still leaving access to the inside of the container. Fill the container with growing medium: clay pellets and soil, with wood moss on top, to within ½ inch (1 cm) of the top.

Lift up the container, gently pressing the mesh until it is resting on the moss. Mind your hands when the wires come out through the back. If necessary, rework the edges a bit so that the mesh perfectly covers the soil. Finally, delicately pull the wires from behind; the growing medium must be well maintained but not crushed. Twist the wires together to seal the cage: 9 o'clock with 3 o'clock, 10 o'clock with 5 o'clock, and 2 o'clock with 7 o'clock.

SELECTED PLANTS

- Woolly thyme (*Thymus pseudolanuginosus*) creeps outward vigorously, hanging down 12 to 16 inches (30–40 cm), and spreading out over a width of 12 inches (30

To satisfy the chef or the cook, and all the food lovers of the household, here's a circle of thyme to hang on the wall near the kitchen window, on your balcony or terrace.

cm). Its gray-green, very hairy foliage is delightful. Its flowers are pink.

- Wild thyme (*Thymus serpyllum*), is very aromatic, with green foliage taking on red tones when there is a lot of sunshine. It spreads out and hangs down slightly, and produces purplish-pink flowers.

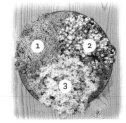

1. Thyme *serpyllum*
2. Thyme *serpyllum* 'Albus'
3. Thyme *pseudolanuginosus*

Different shapes

Although it is circular here, the container could be square, rectangular, or oval. You simply have to think about spacing the plants in a staggered way, at equal distances.

- The *Thymus serpyllum* 'Albus' variety has white flowers that stand out elegantly against the intense green foliage.

LOCATION

Exposure: Sun.

Position: This aromatic "plant picture" can be hung anywhere, preferably close to the house so that it is within easy reach when you are cooking—but you could also hang it on the garden shed or the wall of the vegetable garden.

PLANTING

When to plant: All year.

How to plant: Place the container horizontally. Soak the potted plants for one minute in a basin of water. Remove some of the earth from around the roots, and then place the plants so you can judge the effect. Both of the wild thyme varieties are placed on the same level, 4 inches (10 cm) from the upper part of the circle, and 5 inches (12 cm) apart. The woolly thyme is placed centrally, underneath, 5 inches (12 cm) below the line of the two wild thymes. To plant, cut the wire mesh in the chosen places with a small pair of wire cutters; remove the excess moss, push the earth aside to leave enough room for the roots, and install the plants. Fill in again, using a fork and small spoon for these operations. Tamp down as much as possible, moisten the earth with a mist spray, and then put the moss back on top of the earth to help wedge the whole thing in place. Put back the cut edges of the wire mesh as close as possible to each plant.

Above: *Thymus pseudolanuginosus.*

Opposite: *Thymus serpyllum.*

MAINTENANCE

Twice a week, or more often if the weather is very hot, take down the container, place it flat on a table, and, using a spray, mist the growing medium with water at ambient temperature. Wait a few minutes before hanging it up again.

HARVEST

Thymes are very decorative with their evergreen foliage, and turn into carpets of flowers from June to August. You can cut off little branches as you need them with a small pair of scissors, throughout the year, even—or, rather, particularly—when the plants are flowering.

LIFESPAN

Three months, six months, or sometimes a year . . . It all depends on how the soil is massing together, and on watering, which is not always easy to manage. In the meantime, take full advantage of this pretty picture that you can eat! Very soon after planting, within a month, the thymes will establish themselves and start to hang down gracefully.

When the plants start to show signs of weakness, replant them in normal pots or directly in the soil in the garden.

CONVENTIONAL
IN-GROUND PLANTING

It is very easy to succeed when you plant in open ground, so long as you take account of orientation and the soil when you choose your plants. Follow up with adequate watering, attach the plant to its support, prune it correctly, and there you are. Dare to be original!

SCREEN OF WINTER JASMINE

Plants
- 3 winter jasmines
- Packets of annual seeds

Materials
- 4 thick wooden posts, 9 feet (2.7 m) tall
- Thick wire
- Compost

TECHNIQUE

To make a screen of three panels (which could also consist of just one or two panels), place your four posts in a staggered pattern 3 feet (1 m) apart, in front of the place you want to hide. Drive them well into the ground using a heavy mallet, to a depth of 20 to 27.5 inches (50–70 cm). Link them together with taut wire; every 12 or 16 inches (30 or 40 cm), starting from the top.

PREPARATION TIME
2 HOURS

If you want to hide an unsightly corner, such as the compost or the garbage, why not install a screen covered with climbing plants? Stylish, inexpensive, and easy to put in place . . . so there's no reason to hesitate!

Sunshine!

Jasmine is well able to tolerate partial shade, but all annual climbers need sunshine in order to flourish. It is therefore better to choose a sunny position for your screen if you can.

SELECTED PLANTS

Winter jasmine, or *Jasminium nudiflorum*, can grow 10 to 13 feet (3–4 m) tall, but it is easy to keep it to the height you want. It will tolerate any situation, from full sun to shade, where it will still produce flowers. The elegant dark green evergreen foliage is a background for small yellow flowers, which are not scented, but this doesn't matter: they bring a bit of winter sunshine! In addition, it is easy to train annual climbers to grow up it and bloom during the summer (sweet peas, morning glory, climbing nasturtiums, Black-eyed Susan vine, etc.):

- For light but ever-present scents, sow sweet peas from April on; the summer flowers are in pink, mauve, purple, and white tones.

- *Ipomoea* (morning glory) plants are delightful creepers with big, spectacular trumpet-shaped flowers in sumptuous colors: all the tones of blue and purple, white, pink, violet . . . Sow them directly in late May, in seed holes 20 inches (50 cm) apart, and they will bloom from July until the first frosts.

- Climbing nasturtiums have single or double flowers, all of them in orange

tones. You can pick them whenever you want and add them, with their incomparable peppery taste, to your salads. Sow them directly in the ground from early May, 28 inches (70 cm) apart.

   - Wait until there is no longer any risk of frost before you sow Black-eyed Susan vine (*Thunbergia alata*). Its single flowers, with a characteristic dark spot in the center, are orange, yellow, or straw-colored.

   - For something a little more unusual, sow seeds of *Mina lobata* (Spanish flag) in late May. Its orange tubular flowers form upright clusters.

LOCATION

Exposure: Sun or partial shade.
Position: Designed as a screen to hide an unsightly place, this installation could also serve to enclose a vegetable garden, or the children's play corner, or to hide a rainwater tank.

PLANTING

When to plant: In autumn or spring.
How to plant: In front, and at the center of each panel, dig a hole 16 inches (40 cm) in all directions, put in a couple of handfuls of compost, and then plant the jasmines. Fill in and water liberally.

MAINTENANCE

- As the branches of the jasmine grow, attach them to the wire frame with raffia.

   - In the first year after planting, water every week from May to September.

   - Winter jasmine needs hardly any pruning, but if some of the branches become unruly or unattractive, you can cut them back after the end of flowering, in April.

   - Every year, in April, sow the annuals you have chosen, directly in the ground, making holes 1 to 1.5 inches (3–4 cm) deep and putting three seeds in each hole: a single variety or a mixture according to

your own taste and the scheme of your garden. Remember to soak harder seeds overnight before planting them in the ground.

FLOWERING
Winter jasmine flowers from November to March. Flowering stops if the weather gets very cold, but starts again as soon as there is the slightest thaw. The annuals start to bloom in June, and will continue until the first frosts, particularly if you plant several different varieties.

LIFESPAN
This installation will still be there in twenty years' time!

Opposite: Black-eyed Susan vine.
Top left: *Jasminium nudiflorum.*
Above, from top to bottom: *Mina lobata*, morning glory.

SPOTTED TAPESTRY

Plants
1 climbing hydrangea,
Hydrangea petiolaris

Materials
- Leaf mold
- Compost

TECHNIQUE

Practically nothing to do: the climbing hydrangea clings on all by itself using its crampons, or aerial roots. You can help it, all the same, by guiding it toward the wall at the beginning.

SELECTED PLANTS

Hydrangea petiolaris is very hardy; it grows perfectly well in shade, and hangs onto its vertical support without assistance, using aerial roots. It requires no pruning, and is never sick. Its compact foliage is adorned with flat-topped inflorescences in June. These corymbs still look pretty when they fade, and the leaves take on a lovely golden color in autumn before they fall. In winter, you are left with a lacy network of red stems clinging onto the support. This climber does not grow much during the first two years after planting, but then it quickly takes off, reaching a height of 16.5 to 23 feet (5–7 m) and a width of 13 to 16.5 feet (4–5 m).

LOCATION

Exposure: North- or west-facing; full or partial shade.
Position: *Hydrangea petiolaris* is perfect for decorating a large shaded wall, and will cover a surface of around 82 square feet (25 m²). You could also plant it at the foot of a tree, which it will colonize within a few years; or you can even use it as ground cover in a shrubbery.

PLANTING

When to plant: In spring or autumn.
How to plant: Hydrangeas like deep, cool, humid, non-alkaline soil. Dig a hole 16 inches (40 cm) in all directions, 16 inches (40 cm) away from the wall, add leaf mold and a handful of compost, and plant the hydrangea in the hole. Water liberally and add mulch.

PREPARATION TIME
1 HOUR

Like a warm, cozy coat protecting the wall, climbing hydrangea blooms with ivory-colored inflorescences that stand out, like white spots on a dark tapestry, against the plant's sumptuous deep green foliage.

MAINTENANCE
Climbing hydrangeas require very little maintenance, except for the application of compost every year at the end of the winter. At the same time you can cut off any branches that are getting in the way, as well as any dead ones.

FLOWERING
Climbing hydrangeas flower from June to September, with flat-topped inflorescences that have tiny fertile flowers at the center, surrounded by much larger sterile florets.

LIFESPAN
Will last for decades.

. . . And why not plant *Schizophragma?*
You can replace *Hydrangea petiolaris* with *Schizophragma hydrangeaoides* or *Schizophragma integrifolium*:

- *S. hydrangeaoides* is very similar to *H. petiolaris*: it can grow to a height of 20 to 26 feet (6–8 m) and a width of 16 to 20 feet (5–6 m). Its corymbs are even more spectacular than those of the climbing hydrangea, because the flat inflorescences have the additional embellishment of beautiful white bracts, perched on stalks. Its oval leaves grow over 4 inches (10 cm) long. There is a variety with linden-like, velvety leaves (*S.* 'Moonlight') and another with pink bracts (*S.* 'Roseum').

- *S. integrifolium* is 20 feet (6 m) tall and 10 feet (3 m) wide. Its magnificent inflorescences grow to over 12 inches (30 cm) in diameter. It is not, however, completely hardy: it can only stand temperatures down to 10°F (-12°C), so should only be grown in milder and coastal zones.

SCENTED COLUMN

Plants
1 *Trachelospermum jasminoides*
or 1 *Trachelospermum asiaticum*

Materials
- Chicken wire
- Wire
- Compost

Other names for Trachelospermum
You often find trachelospermum sold in garden centers as star jasmine or confederate jasmine, or sometimes as *Rhyncospermum.*

PREPARATION TIME
2 HOURS

Looking for a way to hide a support pillar or a post? If you plant a *Trachelospermum jasminoides* at its base, it will take over the column, dress it up, make it smell good . . . and disguise it!

TECHNIQUE

Obtain some fine wire netting, such as chicken wire, that is easy to shape. Cover the pillar you want to disguise with a regular layer of this netting, keeping it about 1 inch (2 cm) away from the pillar to leave room for the stems to grow through it. The chicken wire should completely cover up the pillar. Fix it in place using wire.

SELECTED PLANTS

Trachelospermum jasminoides (star jasmine): This evergreen climber can grow up to 20 to 23 feet (6–7 m) in height. It has thick, glossy oval evergreen leaves that are dark green and take on red and brick colors in winter. There a variegated variety: *T.* 'Variegatum', less hardy.

- *Trachelospermum asiaticum* (Chinese jasmine or yellow star jasmine): This trachelospermum is slightly less hardy than its close relative, only tolerating temperatures down to 14°F (-10°C), or 10°F (-12°C) once it is well established.

LOCATION

Exposure: Sunny.
Position: Trachelospermum will tolerate temperatures down to 10°F (-12°C) or even 5°F (-15°C), but hates cold prevailing winds.

PLANTING

When to plant: In April or May, to allow the plant to become well established during the summer.
How to plant: Plant the star jasmine, directly in the ground or in a large container, on the sunny side of the pillar and as close as possible to it, in a hole 16 inches (40 cm) in all directions. It likes a light, non-alkaline, consistent soil, and does not like to be too damp in winter; if the soil is not sufficiently well drained, put a good layer of gravel in the bottom of the hole. Add a handful of compost to the original earth. Water liberally.

Why not ivy?

You can replace the trachelospermum with ivy, which you can find in a multitude of varieties. Choose one with very small leaves, whether variegated or not. But you won't, of course, have any scent or any flowers. In a mild climate, where the temperature never goes down below 14°F (-10°C), *Muehlenbeckia complexa* (maidenhair vine), with its tiny semi-deciduous leaves, will weave in and out of the chicken wire with its tendrils, and grows rapidly.

MAINTENANCE

Trachelospermum requires little maintenance and care:
- Keep it well watered during the first summer after planting, and put down mulch.
- Train the star jasmine toward its support, gradually weaving it into the mesh as it grows, and tie the branches in place with raffia.
- Cut off any unruly branches; the plant should form a sheath around the pillar, so that the pillar can be forgotten. The goal is to end up with a column of greenery.

FLOWERING

Trachelospermum flowers from May to August:
- *Trachelospermum jasminoides*: Delightful little star-shaped ivory-colored flowers, strongly scented without being as heady as true jasmine, appear from late spring to midsummer.
- *Trachelospermum asiaticum*: Its straw-yellow flowers are pretty, but tend to droop and so do not stand out very well, and the flowering period is short.

LIFESPAN

This composition will last for many years, so long as the plant is not killed by an exceptionally hard frost.

GRID FOR A LARGE WALL

Plants
Small-leafed ivies or
Muehlenbeckia complexa
or *Ficus pumila*

Materials
- Galvanized wire
- Metal spikes
- Level
- Chalk for marking
- Compost

TECHNIQUE

The idea is to use plants to make large squares or rectangles on the wall, like a giant grid. To look spectacular, these squares must be 24 to 30 inches (60–80 cm) high. Measure the height of your wall and calculate how many squares you can put on it vertically: two, three, or even four if the wall is very high. Then trace a grid over the entire height and length, using chalk. If your wall is very long, choose rectangles rather than squares. Stand back to judge the effect. If the result satisfies you, install the wire following the marks, using a level to make sure the lines are properly straight and horizontal. Fix in place with metal spikes.

SELECTED PLANTS

The choice of plant (which has to be of just one variety) is based on two main criteria: the leaves must be small, and they must be evergreen.

- Small-leafed ivies are available in a very large number of varieties: sharply cut out, heart-shaped, plain, variegated, spotted, or veined with yellow or white. They can be grown in all regions, even the coldest.
- *Muehlenbeckia complexa* (maidenhair vine) is capable of tolerating temperatures as cold as 5°F (-15°C) once it is well established. Plant it in well-drained soil, sheltered from cold winds, and protect the stock during its first two winters with a litter of dead leaves or bracken, if you do not live in a region with a mild climate.
- *Ficus pumila* (creeping fig) is hardy only in temperatures down to 23°F (-5°C) or 20°F (-7°C) if the soil is well drained and the wall is sheltered from the wind. It should be grown only in milder and coastal zones.

LOCATION

Exposure: Gentle sun, partial shade, shade.
Position: This principle can be adapted to

PREPARATION TIME
4 HOURS

Not sure how to decorate that big wall surrounding your garden? Put green squares on it, which can be developed and refined over the years.

any blind wall, whether it is long, perhaps enclosing a garden, or high, like the gable of a house or barn—depending, of course, on the whether it is possible to plant in the soil at the foot of the wall. As suitable plants can tolerate partial shade, or even full shade, this would be an ideal solution for decorating a corridor between two buildings.

PLANTING
When to plant: In spring.
How to plant: At the bottom of each vertical wire, make a hole 16 inches (40 cm) in all directions. Loosen the soil in the bottom and mix two handfuls of compost with the earth. Soak each plant container for five minutes in a bucket of water. Take out the root balls and plant one in each hole; fill in and water.

MAINTENANCE
Upkeep should be done very regularly:
  - Be sure to water regularly during the first summer after planting.
  - Fix the stems to the wire, so as to form a vertical line. When the plant reaches an intersection, continue to guide the central branches straight upward and train the lateral ones outward onto the horizontal wires on each side, until they join up with those from the next square along. Do this on each level.
  - Cut off any unruly stems.
  - If the stems are not very bushy when they reach an intersection, pinch them out to encourage them to grow more branches. This will prolong the time it takes to get established, but you will quickly be able to see the results.
  - If, after a particularly cold winter, some of the branches have been damaged, cut them back to the first green shoot.

LIFESPAN
With regular maintenance (training and pruning), these installations can last for many years. But a particularly hard winter can destroy them if you have chosen *Muehlenbeckia complexa* or *Ficus pumila.*

WALL OF VEGETABLES

Plants
- Seeds of climbing peas and beans
- Young plants of tomatoes, zucchini, and climbing squash
- Seeds of calendula (pot marigold), love-in-a-mist, and nasturtiums

Materials
- Galvanized wire and metal spikes, or trellis
- Compost

1. Climbing pea
2. Tomato
3. Climbing squash
4. Climbing bean
5. Annuals

The virtues of the nettle
Put chopped nettle leaves in the bottom of each hole when you plant tomatoes: not only are nettles a good fertilizer, but they also repel parasites.

PREPARATION TIME
2 HOURS

In the vegetable garden or even the ornamental garden, if you have a blank wall that is in the sun for most of the day, why not grow vegetables up it? They will be so easy to pick.

TECHNIQUE

Stretched horizontal wires every 12 inches (30 cm), fixed with metal spikes, are perfect for this, so long as they are secured 1 inch (3 cm) from the wall. Every 20 inches (50 cm), fix vertical wires.

Another slightly more expensive possibility is to install trelliswork, also secured at a small distance from the wall. This has the advantage of looking decorative, even in winter when there is nothing growing.

SELECTED PLANTS

- Peas produce straight or curved pods that can be yellow, green, or purple, depending on the variety, containing round peas that are either smooth or wrinkled. We recommend the following: for smooth climbing garden peas, 'Serpette d'Auvergne', 'Express à longues cosses', and 'Roi des conserves'; for wrinkled climbing garden peas, 'Sénateur', 'Telephone', 'À rame', 'Roi des Halles', and 'Maxigolt à longue cosse'; for climbing mangetout peas, 'Géant à larges cosses', 'Super-mangetout Tézier', and 'Géant suisse'.

- Here are our favorite climbing bean varieties. Green beans (or string beans, where the whole pod is eaten): 'Perfection blanc', 'Phénomène à rames', 'Saint-Fiacre à rames', 'Oeil-de-perdrix à rames'; beans for shelling: 'Coco rouge de Prague', 'Soissons vert à rames', 'De Soissons blanc à rames', 'Tarbais', 'Crochu de Montmagny'.

- Tomatoes make people want to start collections—there is such a wide diversity of them: smaller than a cherry or like a big balloon, round, flat, pear-shaped, or misshapen, they come in all kinds of shapes. The colors are amazing, too: red, yellow, orange, green, purple, pink, white, almost black, streaked, spotted, marbled . . . there are nearly two thousand different varieties. Cherry tomatoes do particularly well when grown against a wall like this.

- Zucchini can be long or round, green or yellow, mottled, striped; try out new varieties—the catalogs are full of them! Some have a nutty taste; others are sweet and almost sugary. Among our favorites are 'Black Beauty', 'Rond de Nice', and 'Coutors'.

- You can find more and more astonishing varieties of squashes in garden centers and plant fairs these days: spaghetti squash, 'Jack be Little', 'Pomme d'Or', pattypan, butternut, red kuri squash . . . All have different tastes and uses.

- Calendulas (pot marigolds) are annuals that will seed themselves if they like the conditions. They are normally found in golden yellow or orange, but for more unusual ones, why not have a look through some seed catalogs? You will find them in colors of buff, ochre, pale yellow, ivory, rust, and more. Their petals look exqui-

Good associations
Put in some bedding plants of French marigolds among the annual seedlings, for they will help protect the beans as well as the tomatoes. You could also put in some savory: this aromatic plant protects beans from rootworm.
Plant the squashes close to the beans: they have a mutually beneficial effect on one another.

site when you scatter them over salads or a dish of beans; and calendulas, like French marigolds, are also very useful in the vegetable garden because secretions from their roots kill the nematode worms that attack many vegetables.

- Love-in-a-mist (*Nigella damascena*) is a beautiful annual with graceful blue flowers that bloom all summer and reseed themselves abundantly the following year. The seeds can be used to flavor breads, patties, and cakes of all kinds.

- Nasturtiums are pretty, and they attract aphids, keeping them away from the vegetables; nasturtiums, too, can be eaten, provided of course that they are not covered in aphids, which are particularly attracted by very bright colors. Sow different ones: pale yellow, dark purple, orange, etc.

LOCATION
Exposure: Sun.
Position: Wherever you have a sunny wall with the possibility of planting at the foot of it, you can plant this vegetable garden; even on a patio. It is an elegant and original way to grow vegetables in a restricted space.

PLANTING
When to sow: Sow beans and peas in early May, and sow the annuals at the same time. Put in the tomato, squash, and zucchini plants after May 15.
How to sow: Dig over and prepare the soil to a width of 28 inches (70 cm) in front of the wall. It should be fresh, light-textured, and friable, rich in humus, and not too alkaline. In early May, the day before sowing, soak the bean and pea seeds in a bowl of

lukewarm water. Sow the peas directly in the ground, five or six per seed hole, 16 inches (40 cm) apart. Do the same for the beans, but at the completely opposite end of the wall, as peas and beans do not get on well together. Water well. After May 15, plant the tomatoes and squashes, spacing the tomatoes 20 inches (50 cm) apart and the zucchini and squashes 40 inches (1 m). Put down mulch. Scatter a mixture of the annual seeds, all along the wall. Rake over the surface to lightly cover them, and then water.

MAINTENANCE
- Hoe the peas and beans, but just around the foot of each plant, to avoid disturbing the annuals.

- After the seedlings have come up, wait until the young plants are 6 to 8 inches (15–20 cm) tall, and then earth up around the stalks.

- Water regularly, particularly the squashes, taking care not to wet the foliage.

- As the plants grow, attach their stems to the support with raffia.

- Thin out the annuals to 5 or 6 inches (12 or 15 cm) apart.

HARVEST
- Pick green beans when they have grown to half of their full size.

- String beans can be picked until the seeds start to form inside them.

- Pick fresh beans for shelling when the pods are full and well formed.

- Beans for drying should be picked when they are fully ripe. Pick the pods when they are green and the beans are well-formed inside them.

- Mangetout peas should be picked when the seeds start to form inside them.

- Tomatoes can be harvested from late July until October.

- Squashes are picked from September to November.

LIFESPAN
This composition lasts for several months, during all of the growing period until the final harvest. The following year, practice crop rotation by planting the vegetables in different places.

Left, from top to bottom: Nasturtium 'Tip Top', climbing pea 'Early Onward'.
Right, from top to bottom: Climbing bean 'Soissons blanc', love-in-a-mist, tomatoes.

IDEA FOR CLOSING OFF THE VEGETABLE GARDEN

**Plants: for a wall
20 feet (6 meters) long.**
- One Tayberry plant
- One 'Thornfree' blackberry plant

Materials
- Stakes: 3 to 4 inches (7–10 cm) in diameter and 7 feet (2 m) tall.
- Rope: marine rope would be ideal (two and a half times the length of the wall)
- Compost

TECHNIQUE

Plant the stakes 7 feet (2 m) apart, to a depth of 24 to 28 inches (60–70 cm) on sandy ground; on clay soil, 16 to 20 inches (40–50 cm) will be enough. Make holes with a diameter slightly less than the stakes, and then drive the stakes in with a heavy mallet. Wedge the bases of the stakes with pebbles and firmly tamp down the soil all around them. On each stake, fix one rope at 20 inches (50 cm) from the base, and the other at 12 inches (30 cm) from the top. Tighten the ropes, but not too much; they should remain slightly supple.

SELECTED PLANTS

The Tayberry (*Rubus idaeus* x *fruticosus*) is a cross between a blackberry and a raspberry. It is prickly, vigorous, but sensitive to frost at altitude. Its reddish-purple fruits have an elongated shape.

The huge black fruit of the 'Thornfree' blackberry variety are delicious and very juicy. As this plant does not have thorns, it is a good choice for planting in the children's corner or along a pathway where people regularly pass by.

- The loganberry produces pink-colored fruit in June, and then a second crop in July and August.
- The youngberry is thornless and bears reddish-purple fruit.
- 'Géante des Jardins' is perhaps the blackberry with the most pronounced taste; it is prickle-free and has large firm fruit.

LOCATION

Exposure: Sun or partial shade.
Position: This kind of installation lends itself to many uses other than closing off the vegetable garden. It is perfect for hiding an unsightly corner or separating the children's play area from the rest of the garden, but can also be planted in front of a party wall if the neighbor refuses to have plants growing up it, and can be used to

PREPARATION TIME
2 HOURS

There is often a good reason to close off the vegetable garden, either to hide it if it does not harmonize with the rest of the garden, or, conversely, to show it off and impress visitors when they cross the boundary.

separate the ornamental garden from the orchard.

PLANTING

When to plant: From March to May or in September–October if containerized; from November to March if bare-root.

How to plant: Blackberries like soil that is rich, cool, humid, and consistent. Soak the root ball in a bucket of water for five minutes or, if plants are bare-rooted, trim their roots lightly and leave them overnight in a mixture of soil and water so that they are well coated. Make a hole 16 inches (40 cm) in all directions in the middle of two posts directly below the rope. Mix compost in with the earth from the hole. Put the plants in place, leading the branches toward the rope on each side, fill in the holes and water. Cut back branches to 12 inches (30 cm) from the ground.

MAINTENANCE

- In the first year, keep just four or five stems.

- In high summer, if it does not rain, water every week, soaking thoroughly: blackberries hate dry conditions. Mulch the plants with compost, which can then be dug in when autumn comes.

- The giant varieties of blackberry are very vigorous indeed: during the peak growing period, shoots can grow 3 feet (1 m) in a week. Keep a close eye on them, guiding the stems and regularly attaching them to the ropes.

- In winter, cut back branches that have borne fruit to ground level. Put mulch around the new, vigorous stems, carefully spreading them out.

HARVEST

- Tayberries are ready to pick in July.
- 'Thornfree' blackberries can be picked in August and September.

LIFESPAN

This composition will last for many years, as these plants are practically indestructible!

DRAIN DRESSED WITH A CLEMATIS

Plants
- 1 Italian clematis, *Clematis viticella*
- 1 perennial geranium 'Rozanne'

Materials
- Special trellis to hide the downspout (supplied with screws and other hardware), or a set of two plant supports that clip together
- Compost
- Gravel

TECHNIQUE

There is a choice between two different techniques:

- A trellis to hide the downspout: this is very sturdy because it is fixed into the wall, and a system of interlocking elements makes it easy to assemble. The framework consists of a tube 1 inch (2 cm) in diameter and a trellis made of rods 0.2 inch (5 mm) in diameter, in dark green, rust-resistant steel. Width: 11 inches (27 cm); depth: 7.5 inches (19 cm); height: 6 feet (1.8 m).

- Even easier to put in place is a set of two overlapping plant supports, which clip together. They are made of galvanized steel coated with green polyester;

PREPARATION TIME
1 HOUR

There's nothing more inelegant than the downspout from the gutter! So why not dress it up? No need to be a DIY expert to install these supports, thought up by ingenious manufacturers.

each element is 35 inches (90 cm) high and clips directly onto the downspout—diameter 3 to 4 inches (8 to 10 cm). A system of spring clips means that the support does not touch the wall itself.

- If you are good at DIY, you can use one or other of these techniques as inspiration to design and make your own system for hiding a downspout.

SELECTED PLANTS

Even if there are other plants that can be used instead of *Clematis viticella*, this is still the plant we prefer for this purpose. As it dies back to ground level every year, there is no possibility of it growing underneath the roof. It's up to you to choose the variety you want!

- 'Alba Luxurians': white bell-shaped flowers slightly mottled with mauve, with green spots.
- 'Ernest Markham': velvety red.
- 'Étoile Violette': deep purple with an ivory heart.
- 'Madame Julia Correvon': bright red, with curled sepals.
- 'Minuet': ivory, edged with mauve.
- 'Purpurea Plena Elegans': with purple, very double, even frilly flowers.
- 'Venosa Violacea': white veined with dark purple.
- 'Ville de Lyon': carmine edged with purple.

The geranium 'Rozanne' is certainly the best plant to have appeared in the past twenty years. It has won many prizes in Europe. In a year it will extend by over 3 feet (1 m). When it comes across a support (the clematis, in this case), it will thread its way through it, producing flowers that peep out through the branches.

LOCATION

Exposure: Gentle sunlight.
Position: Although it is designed specifically to hide a downspout, this installation can also be put in place around an upright post, pylon, support pillar of a shelter, etc.

A really useful geranium
The foot of a clematis plant should be protected from full sunlight, so it is very useful to install shade at its base. A roof tile is sometimes recommended, but this should be avoided as it tends to accumulate too much heat. Bushy plants, such as hardy perennial geraniums, are perfect for this purpose.

PLANTING
When to plant: From March to May.
How to plant: In soil that is neither too heavy nor too sandy, dig a hole 16 inches (40 cm) in all directions. Spread a layer of gravel at the bottom; add a handful of compost to the soil; put the clematis in place, slightly sloping toward the support, with the stem buried to a depth of about 1 inch (2–3 cm). Fill in, and then water. Plant the geranium 'Rozanne' in front, and water.

MAINTENANCE
- Guide the clematis regularly toward the support at the beginning. Afterward it will manage by itself.
- Prune back the clematis every year in March to 12 inches (30 cm) from the ground.
- At the beginning of winter, when the geranium's foliage goes rusty, cut it back.
- Apply a good mulch of compost every spring.

FLOWERING
- *Clematis viticella* blooms from July to October. It is covered all over with abundant flowers, whose colors depend on the variety chosen.
- The geranium 'Rozanne' produces blue flowers with white centers continuously from June until the first frosts.

LIFESPAN
You can depend on this installation to last for several years.

BICOLOR FRIEZE
TO FRAME A DOOR

Plants
- 1 white *Solanum jasmi-noides*
- 1 mauve *Solanum jasmi-noides*

Materials
- Nylon thread
- Metal spikes
- Compost
- Gravel

PREPARATION TIME
2 HOURS

Your front door immediately sets the tone for your home. If you live in a stylish environment, tell the world about it by planting this elegant and well-managed frieze.

TECHNIQUE

Stretch nylon threads vertically on each side of the door, 24 inches (60 cm) away from it, attaching them with metal spikes, to a height of 16 inches (40 cm) above the door. Stretch another, horizontal thread between the two spikes at the top.

SELECTED PLANTS

Solanum jasminoides (potato vine) is particularly suited to this stylistic exercise, as the young stems are flexible and growth is rapid. You can cut it back quite radically without damaging it if has gone without pruning for some time. In mild winters, the foliage is evergreen and blooming continues. Left unpruned, potato vine can grow to 13 feet (4 m) in both height and width.

LOCATION

Exposure: Sun.
Position: This type of frame is suitable for windows as well as front doors; clusters of little flowers hang down prettily, like embroidery.

PLANTING

When to plant: From March to June.
How to plant: Dig a hole 16 inches (40 cm) in all directions on either side of the door, aligned with the threads. Spread a 2-inch (5 cm) layer of gravel at the bottom, and then mix in two handfuls of compost with the soil. After soaking the root balls in water for five minutes, put them in place, fill in the holes, tamp down firmly, and water.

MAINTENANCE

- Guide the potato vines along the threads. They will cling to the wall and climb up all by themselves.
 - When they get to the horizontal thread at the top, bend some of the branches inward, on both sides, over the top of the door, to encourage the two colors to mix with one another on the horizontal thread.
 - For maximum effect, you must regu-larly eliminate parts of the plant that do not form part of the frieze.
 - In March or April, if branches have become straggly or damaged by frost, do not be afraid of cutting them down to 12 inches (30 cm) from the ground: new, vigorous shoots will appear very quickly.

FLOWERING

Potato vines bloom from April to November.

LIFESPAN

This frieze will remain decorative for many years so long as there is no particularly hard winter. Potato vines get frostbitten and die back at temperatures of below 0°F (-18°C), but will often take off again from the stock.

Solanum jasminoides

DECORATING THE
BASE OF A TREE TRUNK

Plants
- 3 packets of morning
  glory seeds, of a variety
  of colors

Materials
- Chicken wire
- Fasteners
- Soil

PREPARATION TIME
2 HOURS

Some large trees have magnificent bark, but others look naked and dreary at the base. Why not dress them up with some luxuriant vegetation?

TECHNIQUE

Weed and dig over the ground with a hand cultivator to a distance of 20 inches (50 cm) around the tree; then add a 45 quart (50 L) bag of soil. Prepare the ground again, first with the hand cultivator and then with a rake, to make a fine tilth.

Cut the chicken wire with wire cutters so that it loosely encircles the trunk, at a distance of about 2 inches (5 to 6 cm) all around; it should be 6.5 feet (2 m) high and its length should correspond to the perimeter of the tree trunk. Install it around the trunk, raising it 6 inches (15 cm) from the ground to leave room for weeding, if necessary. Attach it lightly if you want to be able to remove it during winter or more solidly if you want it to stay in place more permanently.

SELECTED PLANTS

Annual *Ipomoea* (morning glory) plants come in an extravagant variety of colors: turquoise, deep purple, shocking pink, pale pink, raspberry pink, white, edged, bordered, and marbled.

There is also a perennial *Ipomoea*, but it will only resist temperatures down to 23°F (-5°C). It is an invasive plant; you can grow it as if it were an annual.

LOCATION

Exposure: Sun or light shade.
Position: This arrangement could also be used to surround a water tank, a domestic fuel tank, or a well.

PLANTING

When to sow: May.
How to sow: The day before, soak the seeds in a bowl of lukewarm water to speed up germination. The next day, make holes 0.75 to 1 inch (2–3 cm) deep, every 8 inches (20 cm) at a distance of 4 inches (10 cm) from the wire, and plant three or four seeds in each hole. Water.

MAINTENANCE

- As soon as the seedlings appear, water them if there is no rain. Always remember that the tree will pump a lot of water out of the ground, so you need to keep a close eye on your annuals to keep them from dying of thirst.

- Guide the plants onto the chicken wire at first, if necessary. Afterward they will continue their climb up into the branches without assistance.

- At the end of the season you can let the plants run to seed, particularly if you intend to recreate the same scene the following year.

FLOWERING

Annual *Ipomoea* plants flower from July to October.

Other plants that like climbing up fences
Sweet peas, climbing nasturtiums, cup-and-saucer vines . . . You can grow some ivy on the chicken wire, too; it makes a pretty background for these plants.

LIFESPAN

Morning glories only flower for four months. If you have the space in a barn or garage, you could bring the structure in for the winter and put it outside again the following spring.

There is, however, nothing to stop you creating a similar scene with perennial plants, and leaving the chicken wire in place.

CLIMBERS ON A LADDER

Plants
- 1 small repeat-flowering climbing rose bush
- 1 large-flowered late flowering clematis
- 2 lavender plants

Materials
- An old wooden ladder
- A large terracotta pot: minimum diameter 23 inches (60 cm)
- Potting soil
- River sand
- Compost
- Clay pellets
- Fixing clamps (optional)

TECHNIQUE

Lean the ladder against the wall in the chosen place so that it looks natural, just as though you were about to climb it. Fix it firmly in place: you can use clamps or you can block it by placing the flowerpot in front; in either case, check that there is no risk of it slipping when the plants are growing up it.

SELECTED PLANTS

- Not many roses, whether climbers or repeat-flowering, will put up with being

PREPARATION TIME
1 HOUR

At the back of the garage you will often find an old wooden ladder—a relic of days gone by. If you turn it into a support for climbing plants, it's perfect for brightening up a dull-looking wall!

grown in a pot. Here are our favorites: 'Narrow Water', abundant blooming with small light semi-double roses clustering together in mauvish-pink bunches with a marvelous scent; 'Blush Noisette', with small blush-pink blooms clustering together in clove-scented bouquets; 'Coraline', very free-flowering, with semi-double, apricot colored roses; 'Ghislaine de Féligonde', with bunches of small flowers, orange when in bud, but apricot to pale yellow after opening; 'Climbing Iceberg, with a profusion of light, white flowers; 'Pink Cloud', with large, very elegant raspberry-pink flowers.

- Varieties of large-flowered clematis include 'Snow Queen': white flowers with bluish reflections and reddish-brown centers; 'Comtesse de Bouchaud': flowers tender rose-pink; 'Niobe': dark velvety red flowers with yellow centers; 'Perle d'azur': lavender blue flowers with cream centers; 'Jackmanii': purple flowers with white centers.

- Lavender, with its evergreen-scented foliage and its very decorative flower spikes, is an elegant way of hiding the base of the rose bush and clematis. You can find varieties with mauve, purple, pink, and white flowers; all of them harmonize well with these climbers.

LOCATION
Exposure: Gentle sun or light shade.
Position: There is a place for this flowery ladder on a terrace, against the side of the house, barn, or garage, or against a party wall, if it is high enough.

PLANTING
When to plant: March.
How to plant: Cover up the hole (or holes) in the container with bits of broken flowerpot, and cover with a thick layer of clay pellets. Prepare the soil: four parts potting soil to one part sand. Add a few handfuls of compost. Fill the pot with this mixture, and plant the rose bush at the back, near the

It can be a good idea to sow some annual seeds in the middle of the other plants: sweet peas, morning glory, etc. Be careful with color harmony, though!

ladder. In front, plant the clematis, with the lavender on either side of it to shade its foot. Tamp down gently around the plants, and then water.

MAINTENANCE
- Guide the rose bush onto the ladder. Remove dead heads regularly.
- Let the clematis grow up through the rose bush, and also bring a couple of its branches down in front of the pot.
- In March, cut off any undisciplined branches from the rose bush, cut the clematis down to a height of 12 inches (30 cm) and prune back the lavender to half of its volume, always cutting into green wood.
- Every year, in March, apply a top-dressing of soil and compost.
- Water in summer, preferably with rainwater, whenever the soil dries out to the depth of 1 inch (2 cm).
- Large-flowered clematis can be capricious. If it dries out suddenly, wait a bit before uprooting it; cut it down to the ground instead, and there is a good chance that it will take off again.

FLOWERING
- The rose will flower from June until the first frosts, sometimes with a pause in July and August, depending on the variety chosen.
- The clematis will flower in June and July, with a second flowering in September.
- Lavender blooms from June until the first frosts.

LIFESPAN
This composition can last for several years, so long as the plants are well maintained.

HAZEL BUNDLES FOR ANNUALS

Plants
- Annual climber seeds
- Hazel twigs, from 2.5 to
  4 feet (0.8 to 1.2 m) long

Materials
- Flexible ties (raffia)

PREPARATION TIME
2 HOURS IF YOU HAVE
HAZEL TWIGS TO HAND

Take advantage of the winter to gather hazel twigs in country hedgerows or in your own garden. Make bundles of thin branches and store them out of the rain.

TECHNIQUE

The main idea is to join the hazel branches together to form bundles. The more convoluted the branches are, the more successful the bundles will be. Gather the branches together in your hand, as you would to make a natural-looking bunch of flowers. Make it look stylish, and perhaps a little spooky, like a witch's broom. Hold the branches together, tying them with a flexible tie, such as raffia. Cut off the base with secateurs, straight. Push these bundles into the ground wherever you want to add volume for a few months.

SELECTED PLANTS

There is an enormous choice of annual climbing plants. Here is a small selection of some of those that are less commonly seen in gardens but can still be easily found in garden centers and nurseries: Black-eyed Susan vine, scarlet runner beans, cowpeas, cup-and-saucer vine, *Mina lobata* (Spanish flag), *Asarina,* and *Eccremocarpus.*

LOCATION

Exposure: Sun.
Position: These natural supports are easy to place, to give a vertical boost to beds of perennials, flower beds and borders, and the vegetable garden. Annuals will weave in and out of them naturally.

PLANTING

When to sow: May.
How to sow: Sow the annuals you have chosen in holes 1 inch (2–3 cm) deep, with three or four seeds in each hole, and water them. These large seeds will germinate better if you soak them overnight in a bowl of lukewarm water.

MAINTENANCE

- Water the seedlings when they start to appear, if it does not rain.

For earlier flowering

Sow the annual climbers indoors in early April. Soak the seeds in a bowl of lukewarm water overnight to encourage germination. Sow them in holes, with three to five seeds per hole, in pots filled with a mixture of two-thirds soil to one-third sand. Water the pots, and then place them near a window. When the plants have grown 8 inches (20 cm) tall, pinch them out to encourage them to form branches. Plant them outside when there is no longer any risk of frost.

- Maintenance consists simply of guiding the young plants onto the bundle of twigs.

FLOWERING

Annual climbers will bloom from July until the first frosts.

LIFESPAN

The annuals will flower for a period of four or five months. After this, you can bring in the bundles and store them for next year; or you can burn them in the fireplace, grind them up to use as mulch, or incorporate them into the compost.

STONE WALL WITH A CURTAIN OF AROMATICS

Plants (for two planters)
- 2 trailing rosemary plants
- 2 trailing savory plants

Materials
- Planters 24 to 28 inches (60–70 cm) long, as deep as possible.
- 4 brackets per planter
- Screws
- Clay pellets
- Slow-release fertilizer spikes (3 per planter)
- Soil, with 5 handfuls of river sand added per planter
- Ladder or mini-scaffold
- Hanging basket spray lance

PREPARATION TIME
4 HOURS

The ground is paved on your terrace or in your courtyard, so you can't put plants into it; and yet that stone wall deserves to be dressed up. How about planting from the top?

TECHNIQUE

The idea is to fix planters to the top of the wall. Climb up your ladder to check that this is possible, measure the thickness of the wall and then buy the appropriate planters and fixing brackets. The wider and deeper the planters are, the better the plants will grow, but pay attention above all to the thickness—and therefore the strength—of your wall.

Check that your planters have adequate holes in them, and make a few extra holes in the sides and the bottom, to make sure the water runs out on your side, not the neighbor's side, of the wall. Then fix the brackets to the wall so that they hold the planters firmly in place on both sides.

What about the neighbors?

If the wall is a party wall, ask your neighbors for permission to install your planters, emphasizing that there will be no risk of their falling and causing damage. Make sure that water never runs down their side of the wall.

SELECTED PLANTS

- Rosemary, an evergreen plant, enjoys full sunlight, likes to warm itself against a stone wall, and hates drafts and overwatering. Here are some varieties of rosemary with prostrate habit, which can trail and hang down over 6.5 feet (2 m): *Rosmarinus officinalis* 'Prostratus', with lavender-colored flowers; *R. officinalis* 'Corsican Blue', with deep blue flowers; *R. officinalis* 'Pointe du Raz', with lavender blue flowers; *R. officinalis* 'Capri', with purplish-blue flowers.
- *Satureja alternipilosa*, creeping savory, has evergreen foliage and countless little white flowers that appear in September. It should not be confused with winter savory, which has an upright habit, or with summer savory, which is an annual.

LOCATION

Exposure: Sun.
Position: This decoration can be put on top of a high wall, on a patio, in a corridor garden, or on a low wall in the middle of the garden.

PLANTING

When to plant: From March to May.
How to plant: If you have scaffolding, put everything you need on it before you start, including clay pellets, soil, plants, and the rest. Otherwise, find somebody who can help you by passing you things as you need them when you are up the ladder. Begin with the first planter, and continue until you get to the other end. Put a 2-inch (5 cm) layer of clay pellets into the bottom of each container; fill with soil to within 2 inches (5 cm) of the top. Plant one trailing rosemary in the middle of the first planter, and five trailing savory plants in the next, evenly spaced out with plants placed near each end of the planter. Then plant another trailing rosemary in the third planter, and so on. Make sure, of, course, that the plants are positioned so that they trail down on your side of the wall! Fill in carefully, tamp down, and then add more soil if necessary, to within 1 inch (2 cm) of the edge. Press in the slow-release fertilizer spikes, and water.

MAINTENANCE

- These plants will tolerate dry conditions, so there is no need for constant watering. When it has not rained for several days, water them with a spray lance or wand extension fixed to the end of the garden hose, with adjustable flow control. This arrangement is very practical for watering plants that are high up. This attachment, called a hanging basket spray lance or watering wand, can be found in garden centers and DIY stores.
- Rosemary grows without needing any particular attention. In winter, if the tem-

perature drops below 10°F (-12°C), protect it with frost protection fleece.

- At the end of winter, cut off all damaged branches.

- Reduce the savory plants by half every year in March. Take advantage of this annual pruning to add slow-release fertilizer spikes. Every three years, put on a top-dressing to a depth of 2 inches (5 cm).

FLOWERING

Rosemary starts to flower at the end of winter, and trailing savory blooms in September.

HARVEST

These plants can be picked throughout the year, according to your needs.

LIFESPAN

The older the rosemary plants get, the more magnificent they become, enveloping and taking over the wall with sculptural forms, and hanging down in a curtain that can be over 6 feet (2 m) long. The savory plants will live for many years if they are pruned regularly.

Top to bottom: Rosemary 'Prostratus', rosemary 'Corsican Blue'.

USEFUL ADDRESSES

Note that specific permits may be required to import plants from French nurseries. In the United States, consult the USDA's APHIS website, www.aphis.usda.gov/import_export/index.shtml; in the United Kingdom, see http://apps.rhs.org.uk/advicesearch/Profile.Aspx?pid=435.

MATERIALS

PVC (USA)
E&T Plastics
8 locations nationwide
(201) 257-5110
www.e-tplastics.com

PVC (France)
Weber Métaux & Plastiques
3 stores:
9, rue de Poitou, 75003 Paris
66, rue de Turenne, 75003 Paris
34, rue Maurice-Gunsbourg,
94200 Ivry-sur-Seine
(33) 1 46 72 34 00
www.weber-france.com

Wire/Metal
Direct Metals
www.directmetals.com/

Irrigation Matting
Les Jardins Suspendus
www.lesjardinssuspendus.com

ACCESSORIES FOR FENCING AND HANGING
Gardener's Supply Company
(888) 833-1412
www.gardeners.com

TrellisGardenDecor.com
(724) 513-1852

Natural Yards
www.naturalyards.com

Botanique Éditions
(33) 1 30 54 56 77
www.botaniqueeditions.com

DESIGNERS

Patrick Blanc
www.verticalgarden
patrickblanc.com

Richard Dhennin
http://vegeforme.blogspot.com

READY-TO-INSTALL VERTICAL GARDENS

ELT Easy Green
(866) 306-7773
www.eltlivingwalls.com

Gsky Plant systems
www.gsky.com

Casa Verde®
Lieu-dit La Plante
18370 Châteaumeillant
(33) 2 48 61 34 80
www.lemurvegetal.fr

Wallflore®
www.wallflore.com
Greenwall®
10, boulevard Victor-Hugo
34000 Montpellier
(33) 4 34 76 34 76
www.greenwall.fr

Canevaflor®
13, boulevard Edmond-Michelet
69008 Lyon
(33) 4 37 90 58 54
www.canevaflor.com

Végétalis
Greenwall
www.greenwall.fr

PLANT PICTURES

Dorian Green
Boutique "Les jardins de Lutèce"
7 rue des Patriarches
75005 Paris
(33) 1 45 84 75 13
www.doriangreen.fr

Idées B Création
(33) 3 20 84 95 17
www.idcrea.net

NURSERIES

Clematis (USA)
Donahue's Clematis Specialists
www.donahuesgreenhouse.com

Clematis (France)
Pépinières Travers
45650 Saint-Jean-le-Blanc
(33) 02 38 66 14 90
www.clematite.net

Pépinière des Farguettes (clematis and roses)
Les Farguettes
24520 Saint-Nexans
(33) 5 53 24 37 54
www.pepiniere-des-farguettes.com

Ferns (USA)
Crownsville Nursery
www.crownsvillenursery.com

Ferns (France)
Le monde des fougères
Olivier Ezavin
955, chemin du Puits
06330 Roquefort-les-Pins
(33) 4 93 77 63 38
www.pepinieres-ezavin.com

Perennials (USA)
Hallson Gardens
14280 S Meridian Rd
Cement City, MI 49233
www.perennialnursery.com

Wayside Gardens
www.waysidegardens.com

Perennials (France)
Le Jardin de Campagne
Nathalie Becq
13, rue de Butel
95810 Grisy-les-Plâtres
(33) 1 34 66 62 87
www.jardindecampagne.com

Jardin pépinière La Rosée
Audrey Funten
44320 Saint-Père-en-Retz
(33) 6 34 35 22 10
www.larosee.fr

Ellebore (perennials and climbers)
Nadine Albouy and Christian Geoffroy
La Chamotière
61360 Saint-Jouin-de-Blavou
(33) 2 33 83 37 72
www.pepiniere-ellebore.fr

Le Clos du Coudray (perennials, climbers, and alpine plants)
14, rue du Parc floral
76850 Étaimpuis
(33) 2 35 34 96 85
www.leclosducoudray.com

Pépinières Patrick Nicolas (perennials, climbers, and alpine plants)
8, sentier du Clos Madame
92390 Meudon
(33) 1 45 34 09 27
www.patricknicolas.fr

Aromatic Herbs (USA)

DeBaggio's Herb Farm and
Nursery
www.debaggioherbs.com

Aromatic Herbs (France)

Arom'antique

Laurent Bourgeois

Quartier La Ville

26750 Parnans

(33) 4 75 45 34 92

www.aromantique.com

Ornamental Grasses (USA)

Walla Walla Nursery Co.

www.wallawallanursery.com

Ornamental Grasses (France)

Le Jardin d'herbes

Christine Voland and Didier
Marchand

La Cordonnais

35560 Bazouges-la-Pérouse

(33) 2 99 97 40 85

**Jardin Plume (perennials and
ornamental grasses)**

Sylvie and Patrick Quibel

76116 Auzouville-sur-Ry

(33) 2 35 23 00 01

www.lejardinplume.com

Rock Garden Plants (USA)

Everymay Nursery

www.everymay.com

Rock Garden Plants (France)

Les Rocailles du Val

Christophe Vialle

2, rue de la Croix, 28300 Jouy

(33) 2 37 22 80 58

Roses (USA)

Summerstone Nursery

www.summerstonenursery.
com

Roses (France)

Les Roses Anciennes d'André
Eve

1, rue André Eve

Z.A. Morailles

Pithiviers-le-Vieil

45308 Pithiviers-le-Vieil

(33) 2 38 30 01 30

www.roses-anciennes-eve.com

PHOTO CREDITS

Patrick Blanc
pp. 10-11, 12, 16, 18, 19, 20, 21, 22 t, 22 b, 23, 24, 44.

Noémie Vialard
pp. 26, 27, 31, 33 t, 33 b, 34 tl, 34 bl, 34r, 36, 38 tl, 38 tt, 38 m, 38 b, 39.

Biosptoto
Richard Bloom/GAP : pp. 8 (resiln : Ian Rexter), 83 mr, 100 t, 131. *Mark Bolton/GAP* : pp. 14, 49. *John Glover/GAP* : pp. 15 l, 140 m. *Lynn Keddie/GAP* : p. 15 r. *Rob Whitworth/GAP* : p. 37. *Hervé Lenain* : pp. 51, 75 m, 105 t, 140 t. *Denis Bringard (créateur : Patrick Blanc)* : pp. 58-59. *Elke Borkowski/GAP* : pp. 64 t, 104. *Anne Green-Armytage/GPL* : p. 65 tl. *J. S. Sira/GAP* : pp. 65 tr, 88. *Digitalice* : p. 65 ml. *Geoff Kidd/Science Photo Library* : p. 65 br. *Michel Gunther* : p. 70. *Gilles Le Scanff & Joëlle-Caroline Maye* : p. 71 tl. *Sarah Cuttle/GAP* : p. 71 bl. *Juliette Wade/GPL* : p. 71 br. *Howard Rice/GAP* : pp. 75 t, 83 tr. *Frédéric Didillon* : pp. 75 b, 87 b. *Philippe Giraud* : pp. 78 r, 79 tr. *J.-L. Klein et M.-L. Hubert* : p. 78 l. *NouN* : p. 87 tr. *Pernilla Bergdahl/GAP* : p. 79 br. *Carole Drake/GAP* : p. 82. *Visions Pictures* : pp. 83 bl, 100 b. *Alexandre Petzold* : p. 86 t. *Archie Young/Science Photo Library* : p. 86 b. *FhF GreenMedia/GAP* : p. 87 tl. *Edwards Heather/GAP* : p. 90 b. *Paul Debois/GAP* : p. 91. *Harold Verspieren/Digitalice* : pp. 99, 101

m. *Duncan Shaw/Science Photo Library* : p. 100 m. *Geoff Kidd/GAP* : pp. 101 t, 109. *Suzie Gibbons/GPL* : p. 101 b. *Jason Smalley/GAP* : p. 105 b. *Hervé Lenain & Marie-Pierre Samel (jardin La Bouichère, France)* : p. 108. *Elsa M. Megson/Science Photo Library* : p. 114. *P. & M. Guinchard* : p. 125 tl. *Joël Douillet* : p. 125 tr. *André Simon* : p. 125 mr. *Keith Burdett/GAP* : p. 125 bl. *Michael Howes/GAP* : p. 140 b.

Rustica
Frédéric Marre : pp. 47, 71 tr (Le Bois Pinarr/Marie Marcat), 65 bl (pépinière Relabroye), 65 mr (Lepale), 81, 83 tl (jarrinerie Truffaut), 83 br, 90 t (Lepale). *Christian Hochet* : pp. 48, 115 b (conservatoire re Milly-la-Forêt), 125 br (stylisme B. Ballureau). *Eric Brenckle* : pp. 50 (Llobe Planter), 115 l (école ru Breuil). *Franck Boucourt* : p. 115 t (Bertranr Frères). *Jean Lebret (Clos du Coudray)* : pp. 79 l, 96, 97 br. *Alexandre Petzold (Clos du Coudray)* : pp. 97 l, 97 tr.

Paul-Antoine Levasseur : p. 6.
Accroplant (www.accroplant.com) : p. 57 t.
Wallflore® de PlantOver (réalisation Gally) : p. 57 b.

Cover photo: Noémie Vialard.
Photo du rabat : Pascal Heni.

INDEX

[Page numbers in italic refer to captions or highlighted text.]